# 99 Delicious Danish Pastry Recipes: A Sweet Taste of Denmark

Delici DaniPast

Copyright © 2023 Delici DaniPast
All rights reserved.
:

# Contents

INTRODUCTION ..................................................................... 7
1. Marzipan Traditional Danish Pastries ................................ 8
2. Coconut-Almond Filled Danish Pastries .......................... 8
3. Caramel-Apple Danish Pastries ......................................... 9
4. Chocolate-Orange Danish Pastries .................................. 10
5. Plain Raisin-Filled Danish Pastries .................................. 11
6. Nut-Filled Danish Pastries ............................................... 12
7. Mango-Almond Danish Pastries ...................................... 13
8. Apricot-Raisin Danish Pastries ........................................ 14
9. Raspberry-Cream Cheese Danish Pastries ...................... 15
10. Pecan-Cinnamon Danish Pastries .................................. 17
11. Cardamom Brown Sugar Danish Pastries ...................... 18
12. Mocha-Almond Danish Pastries .................................... 19
13. Lemon-Ricotta Danish Pastries ...................................... 20
14. White Chocolate Danish Pastries ................................... 21
15. Walnut-Cherry Danish Pastries ...................................... 22
16. Blueberry-Ginger Danish Pastries .................................. 23
17. Nutella Danish Pastries .................................................. 24
18. Streusel-Blueberry Danish Pastries ................................ 25
19. Chocolate Hazelnut Danish Pastries .............................. 26
20. Peanut Butter Chocolate Danish Pastries ...................... 27
21. Salted Caramel Danish Pastries ..................................... 29
22. Strawberry-Cream Cheese Danish Pastries ................... 30
23. Apple-Cinnamon Danish Pastries .................................. 31
24. Cream Cheese-Coconut Danish Pastries ....................... 32
25. Jam-Filled Danish Pastries ............................................. 33
26. Toasted Almond Danish Pastries ................................... 34
27. Caramel-Pecan Danish Pastries ..................................... 35

28. Banana-Walnut Danish Pastries .................................................................. 36
29. Jam-Filled Vanilla Custard Danish Pastries ............................................... 37
30. Apricot Custard Danish Pastries ................................................................ 38
31. Orange-Almond Danish Pastries ................................................................ 39
32. Baked Apple Danish Pastries ..................................................................... 40
33. Sour Cream Danish Pastries ...................................................................... 42
34. Whiskey-Caramel Danish Pastries ............................................................ 43
35. Apple-Marmalade Danish Pastries ............................................................ 44
36. Coconut Sprinkled Danish Pastries ........................................................... 45
37. Almond Paste Danish Pastries ................................................................... 46
38. Toffee-Apple Danish Pastries .................................................................... 47
39. Spicy Peach Danish Pastries ...................................................................... 48
40. Chocolate Mousse Danish Pastries ............................................................ 49
41. Raspberry-Vanilla Danish Pastries ............................................................ 50
42. Orange-Marmalade Danish Pastries .......................................................... 51
43. Mocha-Hazelnut Danish Pastries ............................................................... 52
44. Hazelnut-Coconut Danish Pastries ............................................................ 53
45. Chocolate-Cherry Danish Pastries ............................................................. 54
46. Mascarpone-Almond Danish Pastries ....................................................... 55
47. Creamy Custard Filled Danish Pastries ..................................................... 56
48. Apple-Pecan Danish Pastries ..................................................................... 57
49. Coconut-Lemon Danish Pastries ............................................................... 58
50. Chocolate-Almond Danish Pastries ........................................................... 59
51. Hot Chocolate Filled Danish Pastries ........................................................ 60
52. Pecan-Honey Danish Pastries .................................................................... 61
53. Vanilla-Cranberry Danish Pastries ............................................................ 62
54. Coconut-Raspberry Danish Pastries .......................................................... 63
55. Cherry-Chocolate Danish Pastries ............................................................. 64
56. Banana-Nutella Danish Pastries ................................................................ 65

57. Hazelnut-Mocha Danish Pastries .......................................................... 66
58. Apricot-Chocolate Danish Pastries ...................................................... 67
59. Coffee-Cinnamon Danish Pastries ...................................................... 68
60. Orange-Whiskey Danish Pastries ........................................................ 69
61. Walnut-Custard Danish Pastries ......................................................... 70
62. Pecan-White Chocolate Danish Pastries ............................................. 72
63. Almond-Coconut Danish Pastries ...................................................... 72
64. Cranberry-Cream Cheese Danish Pastries .......................................... 73
65. Maple-Pecan Danish Pastries ............................................................. 75
66. Pumpkin-Cinnamon Danish Pastries ................................................. 76
67. Caramel-Pumpkin Danish Pastries .................................................... 77
68. Toffee-Chocolate Danish Pastries ....................................................... 78
69. White Chocolate-Almond Danish Pastries ........................................ 79
70. Matcha Powder-Coconut Danish Pastries ......................................... 79
71. Peanut Butter-Chocolate Danish Pastries .......................................... 81
72. Nutella-Coconut Danish Pastries ....................................................... 81
73. Cranberry-Blueberry Danish Pastries ................................................. 82
74. Spiced Apple-Cinnamon Danish Pastries .......................................... 83
75. Caramel-Apple Danish Pastries .......................................................... 84
76. Chocolate-Mint Danish Pastries ........................................................ 85
77. Coconut-Mango Danish Pastries ....................................................... 86
78. Cranberry-Almond Danish Pastries ................................................... 87
79. Orange-Zest Danish Pastries .............................................................. 89
80. Pistachio-Cream Cheese Danish Pastries ........................................... 90
81. Lemon-Blueberry Danish Pastries ..................................................... 91
82. Passion Fruit-Mango Danish Pastries ................................................ 92
83. Strawberry-Banana Danish Pastries ................................................... 93
84. Salted Caramel Chocolate Danish Pastries ........................................ 94
85. Creamy Custard Coconut Danish Pastries ........................................ 95

86. Nutella-Raspberry Danish Pastries ............................................................. 96
87. Caramel-Walnut Danish Pastries ................................................................ 97
88. Apple Cider-Coconut Danish Pastries ....................................................... 98
89. Honey-Lemon Danish Pastries ................................................................... 99
90. Mango-Coconut Danish Pastries .............................................................. 100
91. Pecan-Cream Cheese Danish Pastries ...................................................... 102
92. Jam-Filled Banana Danish Pastries .......................................................... 102
93. Caramel-Pecan Danish Pastries ................................................................ 104
94. Vanilla-Ginger Danish Pastries ................................................................ 105
95. Orange-Cherry Danish Pastries ............................................................... 105
96. White Chocolate-Pecan Danish Pastries ................................................. 106
97. Pecan-Caramel Danish Pastries ............................................................... 108
98. Blueberry-Cream Cheese Danish Pastries .............................................. 109
99. Maple-Bacon Danish Pastries .................................................................. 110
CONCLUSION .................................................................................................. 111

# INTRODUCTION

Welcome to the world of Danish pastries - a combination of delicious flavors and textures, the perfect treat for any occasion. 99 Delicious Danish Pastry Recipes offers a unique taste of Denmark, bringing the industry-leading recipes and techniques from Denmark's leading pastry chefs straight to your kitchen. Whether you're an experienced baker or a novice, this cookbook has all the information you need to recreate the perfect authentic Danish pastries.

From classic cinnamon and custard swirls to rich yet light choux pastries and crusty glazed tartes, this cookbook includes an array of tantalizing options to make at home. This collection of recipes features traditional favorites and unique variations on traditional classics, guaranteeing something to love for everyone. All recipes are clearly listed with detailed instructions and usage tips, making sure success is easy to achieve.

99 Delicious Danish Pastry Recipes also includes helpful hints and tricks that let you learn the basics of Danish baking, perfect if you're just getting started with the craft. Learn everything you need to know about working with dough, folding techniques, glazing processes, and more, as well as helpful recipes for homemade frostings and syrups. Additionally, this cookbook also provides tips and tricks on presentation and storage, making sure your Danish pastries look as good as they taste.

Whether you're making these treats for your family or to impress friends and relatives, 99 Delicious Danish Pastry Recipes is sure to help you recreate the delicious flavors of Danish pastries in your own home. With a range of specialties and flavors, this cookbook takes the hard work and guesswork out of Danish baking. So, when it comes to making the perfect traditional Danish pastries, this cookbook has all the recipes and tips you need!

## 1. Marzipan Traditional Danish Pastries

Marzipan Traditional Danish Pastries – a sweet and tasty treat for any occasion. Enjoy these Danish pastries at tea time, with coffee or as an after-dinner dessert.
Serving: 6-8
| Preparation Time: 40 minutes
| Ready Time: 1 hour

**Ingredients:**
1. 2 cups almond meal
2. 1 cup sugar
3. 2 tablespoons unsalted butter, melted
4. 2 tablespoons all-purpose flour
5. 1 large egg
6. 1 teaspoon almond extract

**Instructions:**
1. Preheat oven to 350° F.
2. In a medium bowl, mix together almond meal, sugar, melted butter, flour, egg, and almond extract until combined.
3. Grease two 9-inch round cake pans and evenly divide the mixture between them.
4. Bake for 35-40 minutes, or until golden brown.
5. Allow to cool for 10 minutes before serving.

**Nutrition Information:**
Calories: 143, Total fat: 2g, Cholesterol: 21mg, Sodium: 11mg, Carbohydrates: 25g, Protein: 3g.

## 2. Coconut-Almond Filled Danish Pastries

These Coconut-Almond Filled Danish Pastries are the perfect combination of sweet and savory and will add a unique twist to your traditional pastry. Packed with coconut, almond and cream cheese filling, this recipe is sure to be a crowd pleaser.
Serving: Makes 12 Danish Pastries
| Preparation Time: 15 minutes

| Ready Time: 40 minutes

**Ingredients:**
- 2 sheets puff pastry dough
- 1/3 cup cream cheese, softened
- 1/3 cup plus 1/4 cup almond paste, divided
- 2 tablespoons sugar
- 1/2 cup sweetened shredded coconut
- 1/2 teaspoon almond extract
- 2 tablespoons warm water
- 1 egg beaten with 1 tablespoon water

**Instructions:**
1. Preheat oven to 375F.
2. Unfold the puff pastry sheets and cut each one into 6 equal rectangles.
3. In a medium-sized bowl mix together cream cheese, 1/3 cup almond paste, sugar, coconut, and almond extract.
4. Spread a generous spoonful of the filling onto each rectangle.
5. Roll up the rectangles starting from the long side and pinch the ends to close up the rolls.
6. Place the rolls face up on a baking sheet and brush with the egg wash.
7. Bake for 20-25 minutes, or until golden brown.
8. Mix together remaining 1/4 cup almond paste, warm water, and a few drops of almond extract.
9. Drizzle the almond glaze on top of the cooled Danish pastries before serving.

**Nutrition Information:**
Calories: 202; Fat: 11g; Saturated Fat: 4g; Carbohydrates: 20g; Protein: 5g; Cholesterol: 35mg; Sodium: 80mg; Fiber: 1g; Sugar: 6g

## 3. Caramel-Apple Danish Pastries

Caramel-Apple Danish Pastries are a delicious twist on traditional Danish pastry. Combining a sweet apple and caramel filling with a light and flaky pastry crust, this delicious breakfast pastry is sure to please.
Servings: 24 | Preparation Time: 10 minutes | Ready Time: 25 minutes

**Ingredients:**
- 1 package pre-made puff pastry
- 2 apples, peeled, cored and diced
- 1/2 cup brown sugar
- 1/4 cup butter
- 2 tablespoons cornstarch
- 2 tablespoons cold water
- Juice of 1/2 lemon
- 1 cup caramel topping

**Instructions:**
1. Preheat oven to 400 degrees F.
2. Place puff pastry onto a lightly floured surface, cutting into 6 equal portions. Place each portion onto a parchment paper lined baking sheet.
3. In a small saucepan, melt butter over medium heat. Add apples, brown sugar, cornstarch and water. Simmer until mixture has thickened, about 5 minutes. Remove from heat and stir in lemon juice.
4. Divide apple mixture among the puff pastry portions, spooning into center of each. Top with caramel topping.
5. Bake for 13-15 minutes, or until pastry is golden brown and filling is bubbly.

**Nutrition Information**: Per Serving:
Calories: 214, Total Fat: 10.3g, Saturated Fat: 5.3g, Cholesterol: 8mg, Sodium: 153mg, Carbohydrates: 28.3g, Fiber: 1.6g, Sugar: 5.9g, Protein: 2.2g.

## 4. Chocolate-Orange Danish Pastries

Chocolate and orange are a classic combination - this Chocolate-Orange Danish Pastry is the perfect way to start any morning. These pastries feature a light and flaky puff pastry crust filled with dark and bittersweet chocolate and topped with a sweet orange glaze.
Serving: This recipe makes 8 Danish Pastries.
| Preparation Time: 25 minutes
| Ready Time: 1 hour

**Ingredients:**

- 8 ounces frozen puff pastry sheets, thawed according to package directions
- 1/2 cup bittersweet chocolate, chopped

For the Orange Glaze:
- 2 tablespoons orange juice
- 3/4 cup confectioners' sugar

**Instructions:**
1. Preheat the oven to 400 degrees F. Line a baking sheet with parchment paper.
2. Unfold the puff pastry sheets on lightly floured surface. Using a rolling pin, roll the pastry sheets into two 9-inch squares; cut into 4-inch squares.
3. Place the pastry squares on the prepared baking sheet. Place 1/2 teaspoon of the chopped chocolate in the center of each square.
4. Bake for 15 minutes or until golden brown. Remove from the oven and let cool.
5. To make the glaze: In a small bowl, whisk together the orange juice and confectioners' sugar until smooth.
6. Drizzle the glaze over the pastries and serve.

**Nutrition Information**: Per serving (1 Danish pastry):
160 calories, 8 g fat, 2 g saturated fat, 20 mg cholesterol, 71 mg sodium, 18 g carbohydrates, 1 g fiber, 8 g sugar, 2 g protein.

## 5. Plain Raisin-Filled Danish Pastries

Plain Raisin-Filled Danish Pastries are a delightful sweet pastry perfect for any occasion. With a sweet raisin filling encased in light and fluffy pastry dough, these Danish pastries are sure to be a hit with everyone.
Serving: 8
| Preparation Time: 30 minutes
| Ready Time: 1 hour

**Ingredients:**
- 4 oz butter
- 2 Cups all-purpose flour
- 0.33 cups warm water

- 2 tbsp granulated sugar
- 0.5 tsp salt
- 1 tsp active dry yeast
- 0.5 cup raisins
- 2 tsp milk
- 2 tbsp egg

**Instructions:**
1. Mix together the warm water, sugar, and yeast in a small bowl. Let stand until foamy, about 10 minutes.
2. In a large bowl, mix together the flour, salt, and butter until the mixture resembles coarse meal.
3. Pour the yeast mixture into the flour mixture and stir until a soft dough forms. Place the dough onto a lightly floured surface and knead for about 5 minutes. Cover with a damp cloth and let rise for about 30 minutes.
4. Roll out the dough and shape into a 12" x 12" square. Sprinkle the raisins over the dough and roll up into a log. Cut the dough into 8 equal-sized pieces and form into a circle shape.
5. Place the Danish pastries onto a greased baking sheet and let rise for an additional 30 minutes.
6. Brush the Danish pastries with the milk, egg, and a pinch of sugar.
7. Bake in a preheated 375F oven for 15 minutes, or until golden brown.

**Nutrition Information:**
293 calories; 14g fat; 42g carbohydrates; 4g protein

## 6. Nut-Filled Danish Pastries

Enjoy your morning with some delicious homemade Nut-Filled Danish Pastries. These pastries are filled with a sweet nut filling and and delectably crispy on the outside.
Serving: 5
| Preparation Time: 30 minutes
| Ready Time: 1 hour

**Ingredients:**
- 2 cups all-purpose flour

- 2/3 cup white sugar
- 1/2 teaspoon salt
- 1/2 cup butter
- 1/2 cup milk
- 2 teaspoons active dry yeast
- 2 eggs
- Nut filling- 2/3 cup chopped nuts, 1/3 cup brown sugar, 1/3 cup butter, 2 tbsp. all-purpose flour

**Instructions:**
1. In a bowl, mix together the flour, 1/3 cup sugar and salt.
2. Cut the butter into the mixture and add the milk.
3. Dissolve the yeast in a little bit of warm water and add to the dough.
4. Beat the eggs and add to the dough, kneading until it becomes a smooth dough.
5. Cover the dough and let it sit for 30 minutes.
6. In the meantime, prepare the filling. Mix together the nuts, brown sugar, butter and flour until it is lumpy.
7. Preheat oven to 375F.
8. Roll out the dough on a lightly floured surface and cut out desired shapes.
9. Place 1 teaspoon nut filling in the center of each dough shape and fold closed.
10. Bake for 25 minutes or until golden brown.

**Nutrition Information:**
Calories: 283 kcal, Carbohydrates: 29.1g, Protein: 4.9g, Fat: 16.3g, Saturated Fat: 8.2g, Cholesterol: 71mg, Sodium: 191mg, Potassium: 64mg, Fiber: 1.5g, Sugar: 8.1g, Vitamin A: 365IU, Vitamin C: 1mg, Calcium: 29mg, Iron: 1.2mg.

## 7. Mango-Almond Danish Pastries

This delicious Mango-Almond Danish Pastry is sure to make your mouth water with its flaky puff pastry layers and sweet mango-almond cream filling. These delectable pastries make for a perfect snack or dessert.
Serving: 12-15 pastries
| Preparation Time: 30 mins

| Ready Time: 1 hr

**Ingredients:**
- Puff pastry – 2 sheet
- Egg – 1
- Butter – 4 ounces

**Instructions:**
1. Preheat the oven to 350F.
2. Unroll one sheet of puff pastry dough onto a lightly floured surface. Use a rolling pin to roll out the dough until it's about 1/8" thick.
3. Cut the pastry dough into 12-15 pieces using an inverted bowl or a pizza cutter.
4. Place the pieces of dough on a greased baking sheet, so they're spaced a few inches apart.
5. In a small bowl, mix the butter, almonds, mango puree, and almond extract.
6. Brush each piece of pastry dough with the egg wash.
7. Scoop a teaspoon-sized amount of filling into the centre of each pastry piece.
8. Place another piece of pastry dough over the top of each piece of pastry.
9. Crimp the edges of each pastry with a fork, to seal the two pieces together.
10. Brush each pastry with egg wash one more time.
11. Bake in the preheated oven for 20-25 minutes, until golden brown.
12. Let cool for 10 minutes before serving.

**Nutrition Information:**
Calories – 175, Total Fat – 8g, Saturated fat – 5g, Carbohydrates – 21g, Protein – 4g, Cholesterol – 24mg, Sodium – 286mg, Fiber – 1g

## 8. Apricot-Raisin Danish Pastries

Enjoy the comforting flavors of sweet apricots and golden-brown raisins in these delicious Apricot-Raisin Danish Pastries. These pastries are perfect for a leisurely breakfast, snack, or dessert.
Serving: makes 12

| Preparation Time: 25 minutes
| Ready Time: 45 minutes

**Ingredients:**
- 2 1/2 cups all-purpose flour
- 3 tablespoons granulated sugar
- 1/2 teaspoon salt
- 1/2 cup cold unsalted butter, cut into cubes
- 1 egg
- 1/3 cup plus 2 tablespoons cold water
- 1/4 cup apricots, diced
- 1/4 cup golden raisins
- 1 large egg beaten with 1 tablespoon water
- 2 tablespoons coarse sugar

**Instructions:**
1. In a large bowl, combine flour, sugar, and salt. Add butter, and cut in with a pastry blender or fork until crumbly.
2. In a small bowl, whisk together egg and cold water. Slowly add this to the flour mixture, and mix until just combined.
3. Turn out the dough onto a lightly floured surface. Knead briefly, about 1 minute. Form the dough into a disk, and refrigerate for 20 minutes.
4. Preheat oven to 400° F (200° C).
5. Roll out the chilled dough on a lightly floured surface. Cut the dough into 12 rounds. Place the rounds on a greased baking sheet.
6. Place a teaspoon of diced apricot and raisins on each round. Brush the egg wash over the top of each round, and sprinkle with coarse sugar.
7. Bake for 20 minutes, until golden brown. Allow to cool before serving.

**Nutrition Information** (per pastry):
230 calories; 11 g fat; 4 g protein; 28 g carbohydrates; 2 g fiber; 20 mg cholesterol; 123 mg sodium

## 9. Raspberry-Cream Cheese Danish Pastries

This Raspberry-Cream Cheese Danish Pastries recipe is a delicious and unique twist to a classic pasty recipe. This dish is the perfect dessert for an elegant dinner party or a casual brunch.

Serving: 8
| Preparation Time: 30 minutes
| Ready Time: 75 minutes

**Ingredients:**
- 1 (8 oz) package of cream cheese, softened
- 2 tablespoons of granulated sugar
- 1 teaspoon of vanilla extract
- 1 (17.3 oz) package of frozen puff pastry, thawed
- 2 cups of fresh or frozen raspberries
- 2 tablespoons of cornstarch
- 2 tablespoons of cold water
- 1 large egg, beaten with 2 tablespoons of water

**Instructions:**
1. Preheat oven to 400F (204°C).
2. In a medium bowl, combine cream cheese, sugar, and vanilla extract; set aside.
3. On a lightly floured surface, unfold one sheet of puff pastry. Roll pastry sheet to a 14x10-inch rectangle; cut into four 7x5-inch rectangles. Place rectangles on a parchment-lined baking sheet.
4. In a medium bowl, mix together raspberries and cornstarch. Spoon raspberry mixture in the center of each rectangle. Top with a spoonful of cream cheese mixture, spreading evenly over raspberry mixture.
5. Brush edges of the pastries with water. Place remaining sheet of puff pastry on top; press edges to seal. Cut four 1-inch slits in the top of each pastry.
6. In a small bowl, mix together egg and 2 tablespoons of water. Brush egg mixture over tops of each pastry. Bake in preheated oven for 25 minutes.
7. Let cool before serving.

**Nutrition Information:**
304 calories; 16g fat; 37g carbohydrates; 7g protein.

## 10. Pecan-Cinnamon Danish Pastries

This delicious Pecan-Cinnamon Danish Pastry is an irresistible combination of crunchy pecans, sweet cinnamon, and light and flaky croissant dough. With easy to follow instructions, you can make this pastry delight in the comfort of your own home.

Serving: 8
| Preparation Time: 25 minutes
| Ready Time: 1 hour 25 minutes

**Ingredients:**
- 1/2 cup chopped pecans
- 1 teaspoon ground cinnamon
- 1 can of Pillsbury™ refrigerated croissant dough
- 2 tablespoons butter, melted
- 1/2 cup frozen or fresh blueberries (optional)

**Instruction:**
1. Preheat oven to 375F. Grease 8-inch round cake pan with butter.
2. In a medium bowl, mix together the chopped pecans, cinnamon, and blueberries (optional).
3. Unroll the can of Pillsbury™ refrigerated croissant dough and spread it into the greased cake pan.
4. Sprinkle the pecan-cinnamon mixture evenly over the croissant dough.
5. Using your hands, spread the melted butter over the top of the dough
6. Bake in preheated oven for 25 minutes until dough is lightly golden brown.
7. Let cool before serving.

**Nutrition Information:**
Total Serving: 8
Calories: 245
Fat: 22g
Protein: 4g
Carbohydrates: 14g
Fiber: 3g

## 11. Cardamom Brown Sugar Danish Pastries

These Cardamom Brown Sugar Danish Pastries are tender and flavorful with a delicious cardamom-spiced filling and a crispy brown sugar topping. Enjoy a sweet, home-baked classic that can turn any day into a special occasion.
Serving: 12 Danishes
| Preparation Time: 15-20 minutes
| Ready Time: 30-35 minutes

### Ingredients:
-1/2 cup melted butter
-1/2 cup packed light brown sugar
-1-1/2 teaspoons ground cardamom
-1 (17.3 ounce) package puff pastry sheets
-1/3 cup seedless raspberry or apricot jam
-1/3 cup apricot preserves
-1 teaspoon fresh lemon juice
-1 egg yolk

### Instructions:
1. Preheat oven to 400F. Line two baking sheets with parchment paper.
2. In a small bowl, combine the melted butter, brown sugar and cardamom; set aside.
3. Cut each puff pastry sheet into 12 2-inch squares; place on prepared baking sheets.
4. Spread 1 teaspoon of jam in the center of each square.
5. Place 2-3 teaspoons of the butter/sugar mixture on top of the jam.
6. Fold each corner of the puff pastry squares up and over the butter/sugar mixture; pinch the sides together to form a point.
7. In a small bowl, combine the preserves and lemon juice. Brush the tops of the pastries with this mixture.
8. In a separate small bowl, whisk together the egg yolk and 2 teaspoons of water; brush the tops of pastries with the egg yolk mixture.
9. Bake until golden brown and puffed, about 15-20 minutes. Let cool slightly before serving.

**Nutrition Information** (per serving):
Calories: 650; Total Fat: 41 g; Saturated Fat: 20 g; Cholesterol: 75mg; Sodium: 155mg; Carbohydrates: 65g; Fiber: 2g; Sugar: 25g; Protein: 6g.

## 12. Mocha-Almond Danish Pastries

This Mocha-Almond Danish Pastries has it all: a buttery-sweet crust, a creamy mocha almond filling and a crunchy sugary topping! It is the perfect sweet breakfast or dessert that's sure to please.
Serving: 8-10 portions
| Preparation Time: 25 minutes
| Ready Time: 1 hour

### Ingredients:
- Dough:
1. 2 cups all-purpose flour
2. 6 tablespoons butter, cut into cubes
3. 1/3 cup sugar
4. 3/4 teaspoon sal
5. 3/4 cup cold water
- Filling:
1. 2 tablespoons mocha flavored sprinkle
2. 1/2 cup toasted almond, chopped
- Topping:
1. 3 tablespoons sugar
2. 3/4 teaspoon mocha flavored sprinkle

### Instructions:
- Dough:
1. In a bowl, mix together the flour, butter, sugar and salt until crumbly.
2. Add the cold water and mix until a dough has formed.
3. Knead the dough for a few minutes.
4. Cover the dough and let rest for 20 minutes.
- Filling:
1. Place the dough on a floured work surface and roll it out to 1/4 inch thick.
2. Sprinkle the mocha flavored sprinkle and chopped almonds onto the dough.
3. Roll the dough into a log and cut it into 8-10 equal pieces.
4. Place the pieces on a greased baking sheet and let them sit for 15 minutes.

- Topping:
1. Preheat oven to 375F and bake the Danish pastries for 18-20 minutes or until golden brown.
2. In a small bowl, mix together the sugar and mocha flavored sprinkle and sprinkle over the cooked pastries.

**Nutrition Information**: not available

## 13. Lemon-Ricotta Danish Pastries

These Lemon-Ricotta Danish Pastries are a delightful, lemony twist on the classic Danish pastry. Sweet and tender, they are bursting with flavor and make a perfect snack or dessert.
Serving: Makes 6-8 pastries
| Preparation Time: 30 minutes

**Ingredients:**
-1 cup all-purpose flour
-2 tablespoons white sugar
-1 teaspoon baking powder
-1/4 teaspoon salt
-4 tablespoons cold unsalted butter, cut into small pieces
-1/4 cup cold cream cheese
-1/4 cup cold ricotta cheese
-1 tsp. freshly-grated lemon zest
-1 large egg, beaten
-1/4 cup fresh lemon juice
-3/4 cup powdered sugar

**Instructions:**
1. Preheat oven to 350 degrees F. Line a baking sheet with parchment paper.
2. In a bowl, whisk together the flour, sugar, baking powder, and salt. Add the butter and cream cheese, and use your fingers to rub them into the flour until small, pea-sized pieces form.
3. In a separate bowl, whisk together the ricotta, lemon zest, egg, and lemon juice until combined. Pour the ricotta mixture into the flour mixture and stir until just combined.

4. On a lightly floured surface, knead the dough a few times, then roll to a 1/2-inch thickness. Cut into 6-8 pieces and place on the prepared baking sheet.
5. Bake for 15-18 minutes, until the pastries are golden brown. Place on a cooling rack and let cool completely.
6. To prepare the glaze, whisk together the powdered sugar and 1 tablespoon of lemon juice. Drizzle over the pastries and serve.

**Nutrition Information**:
Servings: 6-8
Calories: 239 per Serving
Total Fat: 10.5g
Saturated Fat: 6.2g
Cholesterol: 47mg
Sodium: 142mg
Carbohydrates: 31.3g
Fiber: 0.8g
Sugar: 11.9g
Protein: 4.2g

## 14. White Chocolate Danish Pastries

White Chocolate Danish Pastries are decadently delicious pastries with a delightful filling of white chocolate and a creamy vanilla glaze. Perfect for special occasions, these treats offer the perfect balance of sweet, creamy, and crunchy.
Serving: 10-12 pastries
| Preparation Time: 20-30 minutes
| Ready Time: 50-60 minutes

**Ingredients:**
- 2 cups white flour
- 1/2 cup melted butter
- 2 eggs, beaten
- 1/2 cup cold milk
- 2/3 cup white chocolate chips
- 1 teaspoon of ground cinnamon
- 2 tablespoons of white sugar

- 1 teaspoon of vanilla extract
- Powdered sugar, for topping

**Instructions:**
1. Preheat oven to 350 F.
2. In a large bowl, mix together the flour, butter, eggs, milk, chocolate chips, cinnamon, sugar, and vanilla extract until combined.
3. Divide the dough into eight equal pieces, then flatten each piece by using a rolling pin.
4. Place two tablespoons of white chocolate chips into the center of each dough circle and fold the dough around the chips to make a pocket shape.
5. Place the dough pieces onto a baking sheet and bake in the preheated oven for 40 minutes.
6. Allow to cool and dust with powdered sugar. Serve and enjoy!

**Nutrition Information:**
Each White Chocolate Danish Pastry contains 190 calories, 10 g of fat, 5 g of protein, 23 g of carbohydrates, and 1.5 g of fiber.

## 15. Walnut-Cherry Danish Pastries

This Walnut-Cherry Danish Pastry is a delicious combination of walnuts and cherries in a flaky, buttery pastry. It's the perfect treat for breakfast or an anytime snack.
Serving: 8
| Preparation Time: 15 minutes
| Ready Time: 45 minutes

**Ingredients:**
-1/4 cup of walnuts
-1/4 cup of dried cherries
-1/4 cup of melted butter
-1 package of puff pastry
-1/4 cup of brown sugar
-2 tablespoons of all-purpose flour
-1 egg
-1 tablespoon of milk

**Instructions:**
1. Preheat oven to 375 degrees and line a baking sheet with parchment paper or lightly grease with butter.
2. Place the walnuts and cherries in a small bowl and mix together.
3. In a separate bowl, mix the melted butter, brown sugar, and all-purpose flour together until combined.
4. Unfold one sheet of puff pastry, and spread the butter mixture evenly over it, leaving a 1-inch border.
5. Sprinkle the walnut and cherry mixture evenly over the butter mixture and fold the puff pastry over on itself.
6. In a small bowl, whisk together the egg and milk, then brush lightly over the top of the folded pastry.
7. Place the pastry onto the prepared baking sheet and bake in the preheated oven for 25-30 minutes, until golden brown and flaky.
8. Remove from oven and allow to cool for 5 minutes before serving.

**Nutrition Information:**
Calories: 244
Fat: 14.6 g
Carbohydrates: 24.2 g
Protein: 3.9 g

## 16. Blueberry-Ginger Danish Pastries

Introducing our Blueberry-Ginger Danish Pastries – a delicious combination of sweet and tart flavors. Perfect for an morning or afternoon treat, these Danish pastries are certain to delight everyone!
Serving: 8-10 pastries
| Preparation Time: 45 minutes
| Ready in: 1 hour 30 minutes

**Ingredients**
- 3 tablespoons of butter
- 1/4 cup of white sugar
- 2 tablespoons of freshly grated ginger
- 2 tablespoons of ground cinnamon
- 2 cups of all-purpose flour

- 2 teaspoons of baking powder
- 1/2 teaspoon of salt
- 3/4 cup of milk
- 1 egg, lightly beaten
- 2 cups of fresh blueberries

**Instructions**

1. Preheat the oven to 375 degrees Fahrenheit.
2. In a medium bowl, cream together the butter and sugar until light and fluffy. Add the ginger and cinnamon and mix until combined.
3. In a separate bowl, whisk together the flour, baking powder, and salt. Add the flour mixture to the butter mixture and stir until combined.
4. Gradually add the milk, stirring until a soft dough forms.
5. Turn the dough out onto a lightly floured surface. Knead the dough several times, then pat it out into a rectangular shape about 1/4 inch thick.
6. Spread the blueberries over the surface of the dough, then roll the dough up, jelly-roll style. Cut the dough into 8-10 equal slices.
7. Place the slices on a greased baking sheet and bake for 25-30 minutes, until the pastries are golden brown.

**Nutrition Information**

Calories: 297; Total Fat: 8.7g; Cholesterol: 21mg; Carbohydrate: 48.5g; Protein: 5.3g; Sodium: 121mg

## 17. Nutella Danish Pastries

Nutella Danish Pastries are light, flaky pastries filled with a smooth, creamy Nutella center. Perfect for a special breakfast or brunch, these delightful pastries are easy to make and are sure to be a hit!
Serving: 12 pastries
| Preparation Time: 15 minutes
| Ready Time: 25 minutes

**Ingredients:**

1. 2 cans puff pastry sheets
2. 1/2 cup Nutella
3. 1/4 cup all-purpose flour, for dusting

4. 1 large egg
5. 2 tablespoons cold water

**Instructions:**
1. Preheat the oven to 375F (190°C). Line a baking sheet with parchment paper.
2. On a lightly floured surface, roll out one of the puff pastry sheets to a 12-by-12-inch square. Cut into twelve 3-by-3-inch squares. Place the squares on the baking sheet, spaced 2 inches apart.
3. Combine the Nutella and the egg in a bowl. Spoon 2 teaspoons of the Nutella mixture onto the middle of each pastry square. Gently fold the corners of the square over the Nutella to create a square packet.
4. Beat the remaining egg and 2 tablespoons cold water in a small bowl. Brush the pastries with the egg wash.
5. Bake for 15 minutes or until the pastries are golden brown. Let cool on the baking sheet for 10 minutes before serving.

**Nutrition Information:**
Serving Size: 1 pastry
Calories: 324
Fat: 19 g
Saturated Fat: 6 g
Sodium: 145 mg
Carbohydrates: 33 g
Fiber: 1 g
Sugar: 3 g
Protein: 4 g

## 18. Streusel-Blueberry Danish Pastries

Absolutely delicious and easy to make, these Streusel-Blueberry Danish Pastries will be the perfect treat for your brunch or breakfast!
Serving: Makes 20-25 Danishes
| Preparation Time: 15 minutes
| Ready Time: 45 minutes

**Ingredients:**
- For the dough:

1. 2 cups of all-purpose flour
2. 2 tablespoons sugar
2.5 teaspoons of active dry yeast
3. 2 tablespoons melted butter
4. 1 egg
5. 1/2 cup of warm milk
- For the streusel:
1. 1/4 cup of all-purpose flour
2. 1/4 cup of brown sugar
2 tablespoons melted butter
- For the filling:
1. 1 cup of fresh blueberries
2. 1 tablespoon white sugar
3. 1 teaspoon cornstarch

**Instructions:**
1. In a bowl, sift together flour, sugar, and yeast
2. To the flour mixture, add the melted butter, egg, and warm milk. Knead the dough till it's smooth.
3. Make the streusel by mix the flour, brown sugar and melted butter.
4. Grease a surface and roll the dough out into a large rectangle
5. Spread the streusel over the dough and sprinkle the fresh blueberries.
6. Roll the dough up into a log and cut into smaller danishes.
7. Place each danishes on parchment paper and let it rise for 30 minutes.
8. Preheat the oven to 350° F and bake the danishes for approximately 15 minutes.
9. Let cool before serving

**Nutrition Information:**
Per Serving: 197 calories, 8 g fat (5 g saturated fat), 21 g carbohydrates, 2 g protein.

## 19. Chocolate Hazelnut Danish Pastries

Introducing Chocolate Hazelnut Danish Pastries - a decadent, pastry-style treat which combines irresistible dark chocolate with crunchy hazelnuts, creating a rich and luxurious sweet dessert. Serve this delicious treat at special occasions or when you want something special.

Serving: 8-10
| Preparation Time: 1 hour
| Ready Time: 2 hours

**Ingredients:**
- 2 cups all-purpose flour
- 1 teaspoon sugar
- 1/4 teaspoon potato flour
- 1/4 cup melted butter
- 3/4 cup lukewarm milk
- 2 egg yolks
- 2 tablespoons hazelnuts, chopped
- 3 tablespoons dark chocolate chips

**Instructions:**
1. Preheat oven to 350F.
2. Combine flour, sugar, and potato flour in a mixing bowl.
3. Add melted butter and mix until combined.
4. Gradually mix in milk and egg yolks until a dough is formed.
5. Knead dough for 5 minutes until it is smooth.
6. Cut the dough into 8-10 pieces and roll each piece into a ball.
7. Place the dough balls on a baking sheet lined with parchment paper.
8. Flatten each ball and top with chopped hazelnuts and dark chocolate chips.
9. Bake in preheated oven for 15 minutes, or until golden brown.

**Nutrition Information** (per serving):
- Calories: 143 kcal
- Fat: 7.2g
- Carbohydrates: 15.1g
- Protein: 3.3g

## 20. Peanut Butter Chocolate Danish Pastries

A delicious twist on a classic dessert, peanut butter and chocolate come together to create an irresistibly sweet danish pastry. The crunchy nutty goodness of roasted peanuts, mixed with the delightful taste of creamy chocolate is a divine combination that will have everyone coming back for more!

Serving: 6-8

| Preparation Time: 15 minutes

| Ready Time: 45 minutes

### Ingredients:
1. 2 cups all-purpose flour
2. 2 teaspoons baking powder
3. 1/2 teaspoon salt
4. 1/2 cup cold salted butter
5. 1/2 cup creamy peanut butter
6. 1/3 cup sugar
7. 3/4 cup whole milk
8. 1 teaspoon pure vanilla extract
9. 1/2 cup semi-sweet chocolate chips

### Instructions:
1. Preheat oven to 425F (220°C)
2. In a medium bowl, combine flour, baking powder and salt and mix until combined.
3. Cut in butter and peanut butter until mixture resembles coarse crumbs.
4. Add sugar and mix until combined.
5. In a separate small bowl, whisk together milk and vanilla until smooth.
6. Gradually add wet ingredients to dry ingredients, stirring just until ingredients are moistened.
7. Fold in chocolate chips.
8. On a lightly floured surface, knead dough a few times until smooth.
9. Divide dough in half, shape into a rectangular shape (about 9x12), and cut into 3-inch squares.
10. Place on parchment-lined baking sheet, spaced out evenly.
11. Bake in preheated oven for 15-18 minutes, or until golden brown.

### Nutrition Information:
Serving Size: 1 pastry
Calories: 350
Total Fat: 18g
Saturated Fat: 9.5g
Cholesterol: 30mg

Sodium: 230mg
Carbohydrates: 39g
Fiber: 2g
Sugar: 14g
Protein: 7g

## 21. Salted Caramel Danish Pastries

Salted Caramel Danish Pastries are a sweet and indulgent treat that combine a soft sweet dough and rich caramel. A few flakes of sea salt added to the caramel topping takes this pastry over the top in both flavor and texture.
Serving: 8-10
| Preparation Time: 1 hour
| Ready Time: 1 hour 20 minutes

**Ingredients:**
Pastry Dough:
- 2 cups all-purpose flour
- 1 teaspoon salt
- 3/4 cup unsalted butter, chilled and cut into 1/2-inch cubes
- 1/4 cup sour cream
- 1/4 cup cold water
Salted Caramel:
- 1 cup packed light brown sugar
- 1/2 cup whipping cream
- 3 tablespoons unsalted butter
- 1/4 teaspoon sea salt

**Instruction:**
1. Start by making the pastry dough. In a large bowl, whisk together the flour and salt. Add the butter to the bowl and using a pastry cutter or two knives, cut the butter into the flour mixture until it resembles small peas.
2. Gently stir in the sour cream and cold water until the dough starts to come together. Gather the dough into a ball and turn it out onto a lightly floured surface. Knead the dough until it's all combined. Wrap the dough in plastic wrap and place it in the fridge for at least 30 minutes.

3. To make the caramel, heat the brown sugar and cream in a medium saucepan over medium heat. Add the butter, stir until completely melted, and bring to a boil. Reduce the heat and simmer for about 5 minutes. Remove from heat and stir in salt. Set aside to cool.
4. Preheat the oven to 375F. Roll out the pastry dough on a lightly floured surface until it's thin and rectangular in shape. Cut the dough into 10 4-inch circles. Place circles onto a parchment-lined baking sheet.
5. Place a spoonful of caramel in the center of each pastry. Bake in preheated oven for 15-17 minutes, until golden. Let cool before serving.

**Nutrition Information**:
Each serving of Salted Caramel Danish Pastries contains approximately 353 calories, 19.6g fat, 35.8g carbohydrates and 3.6g protein.

## 22. Strawberry-Cream Cheese Danish Pastries

These delicious Strawberry-Cream Cheese Danish Pastries are a great way to start your morning. They are an easy to make delightful treat that will bring a smile to your face when you enjoy the moist strudel-inspired pastry and sweet cream cheese, strawberry filling.
Serving: 10-12 pastries
| Preparation Time: 40 minutes
| Ready Time: 1 hour

**Ingredients:**
1. 6 ounces cream cheese, softened
2. 3/4 cup diced fresh or frozen strawberries
3. 1/2 cup sugar
4. 1 teaspoon vanilla
5. 2 sheets frozen puff pastry, thawed
6. 1/2 cup confectioners' sugar
7. 2 tablespoons milk

**Instructions:**
1. Preheat oven to 375 degrees F (190 degrees C). Grease 2 baking sheets.
2. In a medium bowl, cream together cream cheese and sugar. Stir in vanilla and strawberries.

3. On a lightly floured surface, roll each puff pastry sheet into a 12x10 inch rectangle. Cut each piece into 12 equal squares.
4. Place a spoonful of filling in the center of each square. Fold each square in half to form triangles and seal edges by pressing down with a fork.
5. Place pastries on prepared baking sheets and bake for 15 to 20 minutes, or until golden brown.
6. In a small bowl, mix together confectioners' sugar and milk until smooth. Drizzle over cooled pastries.

**Nutrition Information**:
Each pastry has a serving size of 2 pieces and contains 193 calories, 10g fat, 19g carbohydrates, and 3g protein.

## 23. Apple-Cinnamon Danish Pastries

Apple-Cinnamon Danish Pastries are a delicious and indulgent treat, combining crispy, flaky puff pastry with sweet and spiced apples. Perfect for any special occasion or a cozy afternoon, these pastries are sure to please.
Serving: Makes 8-10 pastries
| Preparation Time: 30 minutes
| Ready Time: 45 minutes

**Ingredients:**
- 2 teaspoons ground cinnamon
- 2 tablespoons granulated sugar
- 1 Apple, peeled, cored and diced
- 2 tablespoons butter
- 1/4 teaspoon ground nutmeg
- 1/4 cup light brown sugar
- 1/2 cup raisins
- 2 thawed sheets frozen puff pastry dough

**Instructions:**
1. Preheat oven to 400F.
2. In a small bowl, combine the ground cinnamon, granulated sugar, and diced apples.

3. In a medium skillet over medium heat, melt the butter then add the cinnamon-apple mixture and nutmeg. Cook and stir until the apples are tender.
4. Add the light brown sugar and raisins to the skillet and cook for an additional 2 minutes.
5. Cut the puff pastry into 8-10 rectangles and place on a parchment-lined baking sheet.
6. Top the puff pastry rectangles with the cinnamon-apple mixture.
7. Bake for 15 minutes, or until a golden brown crust forms.

**Nutrition Information**:
Serving size: 1 pastry
Calories: 290kcal
Total Fat: 15.7g
Saturated Fat: 8.2g
Cholesterol: 10.3mg
Carbohydrates:31.5g
Protein: 3.9g
Sugars: 16.2g
Sodium: 152mg

## 24. Cream Cheese-Coconut Danish Pastries

Cream Cheese-Coconut Danish Pastries are a delicious combination of sweet and creamy flavors in one flaky pastry. The combination of cream cheese, coconut, and a sweet glaze come together to create a delectably irresistible treat.

Servings: 12 pastries. | Preparation Time: 25 minutes. | Ready Time: 45 minutes.

**Ingredients:**
-1 package (8 oz) of cream cheese, softened
-1/3 cup of powdered sugar
-1/4 teaspoon of vanilla extract
-12 frozen pre-made Danish pastries
-1/2 cup of shredded coconut
-1 tablespoon of milk
-2 tablespoons of melted butter

-2 tablespoons of granulated sugar
-1/4 teaspoon of cinnamon

**Instructions:**
1. Preheat oven to 375 degrees Fahrenheit.
2. In a bowl, combine softened cream cheese and powdered sugar. Mix until smooth. Add in vanilla extract and mix until combined.
3. Next, place Danish pastries on a large baking sheet. Place a spoonful of cream cheese mixture onto the center of each pastry.
4. In a separate bowl, mix together shredded coconut, milk, melted butter, granulated sugar, and cinnamon. Spread the topping over the pastries.
5. Bake in preheated oven for 20-25 minutes, or until topping is golden brown.
6. Serve when cool and enjoy.

**Nutrition Information** (per serving):
268 calories, 16 g fat, 18 g carbohydrates, 4 g protein.

## 25. Jam-Filled Danish Pastries

This delicious Jam-Filled Danish Pastries takes only fifteen minutes of preparation, and around 25 minutes of baking time. This simple recipe makes 8 servings with 324 calories per serving.
Serving: 8
| Preparation Time: 15 minutes
| Ready Time: 25 minutes

**Ingredients:**
-2 cups all-purpose flour
-1 teaspoon sugar
-1 teaspoon salt
-10 tablespoons (11/4 sticks) cold, unsalted butter, cut into small pieces
-1/2 cup ice water
-1 cup raspberry jam
-1 large egg

**Instructions:**

1. Preheat oven to 375 degrees F.
2. In a medium bowl, sift together the flour, sugar, and salt. Add the butter pieces and knead until smooth.
3. Add cold water and mix until a soft dough forms.
4. Divide dough into 8 equal pieces, roll into circles and place on a greased baking sheet.
5. Place a spoonful of raspberry jam in the center of each circle.
6. Whisk the egg in a small bowl and brush on edges of the pastries.
7. Bake for about 20-25 minutes, or until golden brown.

**Nutrition Information:**
Calories: 324
Total Fat: 16.5g
Saturated Fat: 10.3g
Cholesterol: 55.1mg
Sodium: 242.7mg
Carbohydrates: 38.3g
Protein: 4.3g

## 26. Toasted Almond Danish Pastries

Enjoy the rich flavor of almonds in these delightful Toasted Almond Danish Pastries. With an orange-flavored custard filling and a sprinkle of toasted almonds on top, these pastries are sure to become a crowd favorite.
Serving: Makes 12 pastries
| Preparation Time: 25 minutes
| Ready Time: 2 hours

**Ingredients:**
1. 1 package (8 ounces) of cream cheese, softened
2. 1/3 cup sugar
3. 1 teaspoon almond extract
4. 1/3 cup orange juice
5. 1/2 teaspoon grated orange peel
6. 1 package (1 pound) frozen puff pastry sheets, thawed
7. 1/2 cup chopped almonds, toasted

**Instructions:**
1. Preheat oven to 375°. Beat cream cheese, sugar and almond extract in medium bowl until smooth. Beat in orange juice and orange peel. Set aside.
2. Unfold pastry sheets. Place on lightly floured surface. Roll each pastry sheet into 12x9-inch rectangle. Cut each into a 6-inch square. Place on ungreased baking sheets.
3. Place a rounded tablespoon of cream cheese mixture on each square. Top each with 2 teaspoons almonds.
4. Bake for 20 to 25 minutes or until golden brown. Cool for 10 minutes.

**Nutrition Information:**
Serving size: 1 pastry
Calories: 270
Total fat: 18g
Saturated fat: 9g
Cholesterol: 25mg
Sodium: 270mg
Carbohydrate: 23g
Fiber: 1g
Protein: 4g

## 27. Caramel-Pecan Danish Pastries

Delicious, caramel-pecan Danish Pastries are the perfect way to start your day or as a bite-sized dessert. This recipe is sure to tantalize your taste buds with its mixture of sweet and salty flavors!
Serving: Makes 12 pastries
| Preparation Time: 30 minutes
| Ready Time: 2 hours

**Ingredients:**
1. 1 sheet of puff pastry
2. 1/2 cup of brown sugar
3. 1/2 cup of white sugar
4. 2 tablespoons of melted butter
5. 1 cup of chopped pecans
6. 1/2 teaspoon of salt

**Instructions:**
1. Preheat oven to 350 degrees F
2. Line a baking sheet with parchment paper and set aside
3. Cut the puff pastry sheet into 12 even squares and place on prepared baking sheet
4. In a small bowl, mix together sugars, melted butter, pecans and salt
5. Place a spoonful of the mixture onto each puff pastry square
6. Fold up two adjacent corners of the puff pastry to create a triangle, pressing firmly to seal around the edges
7. Place in preheated oven and bake for 15-20 minutes until golden brown
8. Allow to cool slightly before serving

**Nutrition Information** (per serving):
Calories: 204, Fat: 11.5g, Carbs: 23.5g, Protein: 2.6g

## 28. Banana-Walnut Danish Pastries

Banana-Walnut Danish Pastries are a delicious, sweet and easy-to-make pastries made with a fluffy dough base and a creamy banana center, topped with walnuts.
Serving: Approximately 15 pastries
| Preparation Time: 30 minutes
| Ready Time: 1 hour

**Ingredients:**
- 2 cups all-purpose flour
- 1/2 teaspoon baking powder
- 1/4 teaspoon salt
- 1 cup (2 sticks) unsalted butter, cold
- 1/2 cup sour cream
- 2/3 cup mashed banana
- 1/2 cup chopped walnuts
- 2 tablespoons sugar
- 1 egg for egg wash

**Instructions:**

1. Preheat oven to 350F.
2. In a medium bowl, whisk together the flour, baking powder, and salt, and set aside.
3. In a separate bowl, use a hand mixer, or stand mixer to mix together the butter, sour cream and sugar until light and fluffy.
4. Slowly incorporate the flour mixture into the butter mixture, and mix until it resembles a dough.
5. On a floured surface, roll out the dough into a 1/4 inch thick rectangle.
6. Spread the mashed banana over the dough and sprinkle with the chopped walnuts.
7. Carefully roll up the dough, starting from one of the longest sides and forming a long log.
8. Slice the dough into 1 inch thick disks or rounds and place on an ungreased baking sheet.
9. Brush with an egg wash and bake for 25 minutes, or until the pastries are golden brown.

**Nutrition Information**: Per Serving (Approximately 15 pastries): Calories 250, Fat 17g, Carbohydrates 22g, Protein 3g

## 29. Jam-Filled Vanilla Custard Danish Pastries

These deliciously moist and fluffy Jam-Filled Vanilla Custard Danish Pastries are the perfect mix of fruity, creamy sweet flavors that add a tasty twist to any breakfast, brunch, or afternoon tea.
Serving: Makes 24 pastries
| Preparation Time: 1 hrs 45 mins
| Ready Time: 2 hrs 45 mins

**Ingredients:**
- 2 packages active dry yeast
- 1-1/2 cups warm milk (105F to 115F)
- 1/2 cup sugar
- 1-1/2 teaspoons salt
- 1/3 cup butter, softened
- 2 large eggs
- 4-1/2 to 5 cups all-purpose flour

- Egg wash (1 egg beaten with 1 tablespoon of water)
- 1 cup cream
- 1/4 cup sugar
- 2 teaspoons vanilla
- 3/4 cup jam

**Instructions:**
1. In a large bowl, dissolve yeast in warm milk. Add sugar, salt, butter, eggs, and 4-1/2 cups of flour. Beat with an electric mixer until smooth. Add enough remaining flour to form a soft dough.
2. Knead on a floured surface until smooth and elastic, about 4 minutes. Place in a greased bowl, turning once to grease top. Cover and let rise in a warm place until doubled, about 1 hour.
3. Punch dough down; turn onto a lightly floured surface. Cut into 24 pieces. Cover and let rest for 10 minutes.
4. Meanwhile, in a large bowl, combine cream, sugar, and vanilla.
5. Roll each piece of dough into a 4-in. circle. Place 2 tablespoons of jam in the center of each circle; fold in half and press edges together to seal.
6. Place on greased baking sheets; brush with egg wash. Bake at 375F for 15-20 minutes or until golden brown. Serve warm with the whipped cream mixture.

**Nutrition Information:**
Calories 102; Protein 2.1g; Carbohydrates 19.8g; Fat 1.0g; Cholesterol 6.8mg; Sodium 94.6mg.

## 30. Apricot Custard Danish Pastries

Apricot Custard Danish Pastries is a delicious and easy to make pastry treat full of sweet and creamy flavors. These pastries are a great way to enjoy a warm, flaky dessert without spending a lot of time in the kitchen. Serve this decadent dish with a cup of freshly brewed coffee or tea for a perfect breakfast or brunch.
Serving: 8
| Preparation Time: 30 minutes
| Ready Time: 1 hour

**Ingredients:**

- 2 packages of puff pastry
- 2 tablespoons of melted butter
- 4 tablespoons of custard powder
- 1 cup of apricot jam
- 2 teaspoons of cornflour
- 2 tablespoons of vegetable oil
- 1 egg, lightly beaten

**Instructions:**
1. Preheat the oven to 400 degrees F (200 degrees C).
2. On a lightly floured surface, roll out each sheet of puff pastry to about a 10-inch by 10-inch square.
3. In a medium bowl, mix together the melted butter, custard powder, apricot jam, cornflour, and vegetable oil until a thick paste is formed.
4. Spread the paste evenly over both sheets of puff pastry.
5. Cut each sheet into 8 equal sized pieces and place on a greased baking sheet.
6. Brush the top of the pastries lightly with the lightly beaten egg.
7. Bake for 20 minutes or until golden brown, rotating the pan midway through.

**Nutrition Information** (per serving):
Calories: 274, Fat: 15.3 g, Cholesterol: 20 mg, Sodium: 109 mg, Carbohydrates: 31.2 g, Protein: 3.6 g.

## 31. Orange-Almond Danish Pastries

These Orange-Almond Danish pastries are a sweet and flaky pastry filled with orange zest and almonds, bound to have your taste buds singing.
Serving: Makes 8 pastries
| Preparation Time: 45 minutes
| Ready Time: 1 hour

**Ingredients:**
1. 2 cups all-purpose flour
2. 2 tablespoons white sugar
3. 1 teaspoon baking powder
4. 1/2 teaspoon salt

5. 1 cup cold butter, cubed
6. 2 eggs
7. 2 tablespoons orange zest
8. 3 tablespoons cold water
9. 2/3 cup sliced almonds
10. 1/3 cup confectioners' sugar

**Instructions:**
1. In a large bowl, mix together the flour, sugar, baking powder, and salt. Cut in the cold butter with a pastry blender, or two knives, until the mixture resembles coarse crumbs.
2. In a separate small bowl, beat together the eggs and orange zest, then stir into the flour mixture, using a rubber spatula, until it becomes a dough like consistency.
3. Working on a lightly floured surface, roll out the dough to an 8x12 inch rectangle. Sprinkle the dough with almonds, then fold in half lengthwise and roll out again to 8x12 inches.
4. Cut the dough into 8 equal squares. Place the pastries on two parchment lined baking sheets. Bake at 350 degrees for 20-25 minutes, or until golden brown.
5. Transfer to a wire rack and cool completely, dust with confectioners' sugar.

**Nutrition Information:**
Serving size 1/8 of recipe; Calories: 412; Fat 22g; Cholesterol 56mg; Sodium 263mg; Carbohydrates 44g; Protein 6g.

## 32. Baked Apple Danish Pastries

Baked Apple Danish Pastries are an easy and delicious treat for any occasion. These sweet pastries are filled with a delicious baked apple filling and topped with a flaky puff pastry crust to create an irresistible treat. These apple danish pastries are sure to please and make an excellent addition to any table.
Serving: Makes 12 danish pastries
| Preparation Time: 20 minutes
| Ready Time: 30 minutes

**Ingredients:**
- 2 cups all-purpose flour
- 2 tablespoons sugar
- 1 teaspoon baking powder
- 1/2 teaspoon baking soda
- 3/4 teaspoon salt
- 3/4 cup cold unsalted butter, cubed
- 1/2 cup buttermilk
- 2 Granny Smith apples; peeled, cored and diced
- 1/2 cup granulated sugar
- 1/4 cup packed light-brown sugar
- 1 teaspoon ground cinnamon
- 2 tablespoons fresh lemon juice
-Pinch of freshly grated nutmeg
-1 teaspoon pure vanilla extract
-2 tablespoons all-purpose flour

**Instructions:**
1. Preheat oven to 375F with a baking sheet on the center rack.
2. Place the flour, sugar, baking powder, baking soda, and salt into a large bowl and mix together. Cut in the butter using a pastry blender or two knives until pea-sized pieces form.
3. Mix in the buttermilk until the mixture is just combined. Turn the dough onto a lightly floured surface and form into a disk about 1/2 inch thick.
4. Cut the disk into 12 equal slices and lay them out on the prepared baking sheet.
5. In a separate bowl, combine the diced apples, granulated sugar, brown sugar, cinnamon, nutmeg, lemon juice, vanilla, and flour to form the apple filling.
6. Place a heaping tablespoon of the filling into the center of each slice of dough. Gently fold up the sides of the dough around the filling.
7. Bake for 25 to 30 minutes, or until golden brown.

**Nutrition Information:**
Per Serving: 310 calories, 14g total fat, 8g saturated fat, 46g carbohydrate, 2g protein, 3g dietary fiber, 240mg sodium.

## 33. Sour Cream Danish Pastries

Sour Cream Danish Pastries are tender and buttery pastries filled with a sweet but subtly tangy cream cheese filling. These delicious pastries will make a wonderful addition to any breakfast or brunch.
Servings: 8-10
| Preparation Time: 1 hour
| Ready Time: 1 hour and 25 minutes

**Ingredients:**
- 2 packages active dry yeast
- 3 tablespoons white granulated sugar
- 1 teaspoon salt
- Pinch of nutmeg
- 1/4 cup butter, melted and cooled
- 1 cup sour cream
- 4 cups all-purpose flour
- 1 cup cream cheese, softened
- 1/4 cup white granulated sugar
- 1 teaspoon vanilla extract

**Instructions:**
1. In the bowl of a stand mixer, combine the yeast, 3 tablespoons white granulated sugar, salt and nutmeg.
2. In a small saucepan, melt the butter and add the sour cream.
3. Heat the mixture until warm (105-115F).
4. Add the butter and sour cream mixture to the yeast mixture and stir until combined.
5. Add the flour and mix on low speed until the mixture is a smooth dough.
6. Turn the dough out onto a lightly floured work surface and knead until a smooth ball forms.
7. Place the dough in a lightly oiled bowl, cover and let rise in a warm place until doubled in size, about 1 hour.
8. Punch the dough down and roll it out into a 16 inch by 12 inch rectangle.
9. In a separate bowl, combine the cream cheese, 1/4 cup white granulated sugar and vanilla extract.
10. Spread the cream cheese mixture over the dough.
11. Roll the dough up into a log and cut into 8-10 individual slices.

12. Place the slices on a parchment paper lined baking sheet.
13. Bake in preheated oven at 375F for 20-25 minutes, or until golden brown.

**Nutrition Information:**
Per Serving: Calories 360, Total Fat 12g (Saturated 6g, Trans 0g), Cholesterol 33mg, Sodium 284mg, Total Carbohydrate 53g (Dietary Fiber 2g, Sugars 20g), Protein 9g

## 34. Whiskey-Caramel Danish Pastries

This delicious Whiskey-Caramel Danish Pastry is sure to be a hit with your family and friends. Rich, flaky pastry dough is filled with a tantalizing whiskey-caramel filling and topped with a silky whiskey glaze, creating an indulgence that's simply irresistible.
Serving: 8-10
| Preparation Time: 20 minutes
| Ready Time: 1.5 hours

**Ingredients:**
- 1 package frozen puff pastry dough, thawed
- 1/2 cup caramel sauce
- 2 tablespoons whiskey
- 1/4 teaspoon sea salt
- 1/4 cup chopped pecans
- 2 tablespoons whiskey
- 1/4 cup powdered sugar

**Instructions:**
1. Preheat oven to 350 degrees F.
2. On a lightly floured surface, roll out the puff pastry to about 1/4 inch thickness. Cut into 4-inch circles.
3. In a small bowl, whisk together the caramel sauce, whiskey, and sea salt.
4. Place circles of pastry on a parchment-lined baking sheet. Place about 1 tablespoon of the filling in the center of each pastry circle. Top with a sprinkle of chopped pecans.
5. Bake for 20 minutes or until golden brown.

6. In a small bowl, whisk together the whiskey and powdered sugar until smooth. Drizzle each pastry with the whiskey glaze and let cool before serving.

**Nutrition Information**:
Calories: 278
Total Fat: 16g
Sodium: 346mg
Carbohydrates: 25g
Fiber: 1g
Sugar: 13g
Protein: 4g

## 35. Apple-Marmalade Danish Pastries

This delicious Apple-Marmalade Danish Pastry is a perfect way to enjoy a sweet treat. It is incredibly easy to make and the rich, flaky pastry will make you feel as if you've stepped into an authentic Danish bakery.
Serving: Makes 12 pastries
| Preparation Time: 40 minutes
| Ready Time: 1 hour

**Ingredients:**
1. 1/2 cup applesauce
2. 2/3 cup apple marmalade
3. 2/3 cup butter, melted
4. 1 package (17.3 ounces) frozen puff pastry, thawed
5. 4 ounces cream cheese

**Instructions:**
1. Preheat the oven to 400F.
2. In a small bowl, mix together the applesauce and marmalade and set aside.
3. Unfold the puff pastry and cut into 12 squares. Place on a parchment-lined baking sheet and brush with half of the melted butter.
4. Spread a teaspoon of the cream cheese and a teaspoon of the apple marmalade mixture into the center of each pastry square.

5. Fold two opposite corners of the pastry over the filling and press to seal. Brush the pastries with the remaining melted butter.
6. Bake for 25 minutes, or until golden brown.

**Nutrition Information** (per pastry):
Calories: 142; Fat: 8.6g; Saturated Fat: 4.7g; Carbohydrates: 13.5g; Protein: 1.9g; Sodium: 124mg.

## 36. Coconut Sprinkled Danish Pastries

Coconut Sprinkled Danish Pastries are a delicious pastry that combines the sweet flavor of coconut and the classic Danish pastry. For a sweet and flavorful treat, these pastries are the perfect snack. They come together quickly and make a great addition to breakfast, brunch, or a special occasion.
Serving: 8
| Preparation Time: 25 minutes
| Ready Time: 35 minutes

**Ingredients:**
- 500g ready-rolled puff pastry
- 2 eggs, beaten
- 200g desiccated coconut
- 100g icing sugar
- 2 tsp vanilla extract

**Instructions:**
1. Preheat the oven to 180°C/160°C fan/gas mark 4.
2. Roll the puff pastry out on a lightly floured work surface and cut into 8 even pieces.
3. Arrange the pieces on a baking tray lined with baking parchment.
4. In a bowl, mix together the eggs, desiccated coconut, icing sugar, and vanilla extract.
5. Spoon the mixture onto the middle of each pastry piece.
6. Fold the edges of the pastries inwards and pinch them together at the top.
7. Brush the pastry pieces with the remaining egg mixture and sprinkle with extra desiccated coconut.

8. Bake in the oven for 25 minutes or until golden brown.

**Nutrition Information**:
Per Serving: 152 calories; 7.2g total fat; 1.7g saturated fat; 11.6g carbohydrates; 1.9g protein.

## 37. Almond Paste Danish Pastries

Almond Paste Danish Pastries is a sweet, delicious pastry with a unique filling of almond paste. This easy to make pastry is a delicious treat for breakfast, brunch or dessert. It is perfect for occasions like tea parties, birthdays and holidays.

Serving: 8-10
| Preparation Time: 20 minutes
| Ready Time: 1 hour

**Ingredients:**
- 2 (8-ounce) packages crescent roll dough
- 8 ounces almond paste, cut into 0.5-inch cubes
- 2 tablespoons melted butter
- 1/4 cup sugar
- 1 egg, beaten
- 1/4 cup sliced almonds

**Instructions:**
1. Preheat oven to 375F and line a baking sheet with parchment paper.
2. Unroll each package of crescent roll dough and press the seams together.
3. Spread the almond paste cubes in an even layer over the dough.
4. Roll the dough up and pinch the edges to seal.
5. Cut into 1-inch slices and place onto the prepared baking sheet.
6. Brush the top of the rolls with melted butter and sprinkle with sugar.
7. Bake for 18-20 minutes or until lightly golden brown.
8. Brush with remaining melted butter and garnish with almonds, if desired.

**Nutrition Information**:

Serving size 1 pastry; Calories 300; Total Fat 18g; Saturated Fat 7g; Trans Fat 0g; Cholesterol 40mg; Sodium 280mg; Total Carbohydrates 31g; Dietary Fiber 1g; Total Sugars 9g; Protein 5g.

## 38. Toffee-Apple Danish Pastries

This Toffee-Apple Danish Pastries recipe is filled with caramel, apples, and sugar-cinnamon topping to make the perfect, flaky pastry. It's an easy and delicious way to enjoy brunch or dessert.
Serving: 8
| Preparation Time: 45 minutes

**Ingredients:**
- 2 sheets of puff pastry, thawed
- 2 large apples, peeled, cored, and diced
- 2 tablespoons salted butter
- 2 tablespoons brown sugar
- 1 teaspoon ground cinnamon
- 2 tablespoons toffee bits
- 1 egg white

**Instructions:**
1. Preheat oven to 400F. Place the puff pastry sheets on a parchment-lined baking sheet.
2. In a pan, melt the butter and add the diced apples, brown sugar, and cinnamon. Cook until the apples are softened.
3. Cut each puff pastry sheet into 4 equal squares. Place 1 tablespoon of the apple mixture in the center of each square. Sprinkle with toffee bits.
4. Brush each edge of the pastry with egg whites. Fold the edges up around the apples and pinch them together, forming a sealed pouch.
5. Bake for 15-20 minutes or until the pastry is golden brown.

**Nutrition Information:**
Calories: 150
Fat: 10g
Carbohydrates: 20g
Protein: 3g
Sugars: 5g

Sodium: 70mg

## 39. Spicy Peach Danish Pastries

Spicy Peach Danish Pastries are sweet and savory pastries filled with a homemade spicy peach jam. This delicious dish is perfect for a weekday breakfast or brunch, or an afternoon snack. Serve these pastries warm topped with powdered sugar for a special treat.
Serving: 8-10
| Preparation Time: 40 minutes
| Ready Time: 1 hour

**Ingredients:**
-1/2 cup of peaches, peeled and diced
-1/4 cup of white sugar
-1/4 teaspoon of ground cinnamon
-1/4 teaspoon of ground ginger
-1/8 teaspoon of cloves
-Pinch of cardamom
-1 tablespoon of cornstarch
-2 tablespoons of cold water
-1 package of frozen puff pastry, thawed
-1 egg, lightly beaten for egg wash

**Instructions:**
1. In a small saucepan, cook and stir peaches, sugar, cinnamon, ginger, cloves, and cardamom over medium-low heat, about 10 minutes.
2. In a small bowl, combine cornstarch and cold water, and mix into the peach mixture. Cook until thickened, about 5 minutes. Remove from heat and let cool completely.
3. Preheat oven to 375F.
4. On a lightly floured surface, roll out each sheet of puff pastry into a 12-inch square. Cut each sheet into 4 four-inch squares.
5. Place half a tablespoon of the peach mixture in the center of each square. Fold one corner of the pastry over onto the other corner and seal with a fork.
6. Place pastries onto a parchment-lined baking sheet. Brush with egg wash and bake in preheated oven for 20 minutes, or until golden brown.

7. Dust with powdered sugar and serve.

**Nutrition Information**:
435 calories, 19g fat, 54g carbs, 3g protein

## 40. Chocolate Mousse Danish Pastries

A delicious combination of flaky Danish pastry shells filled with a creamy, rich chocolate mousse and topped with a light sprinkle of cocoa powder. The perfect dessert for any occasion!
Serving: 4
| Preparation Time: 30 minutes
| Ready Time: 1 hour

**Ingredients:**
- 8 flaky pastry shells
- 3/4 cup of dark chocolate chips
- 1/2 cup of heavy cream
- 2 tablespoons of sugar
- 2 tablespoons of cocoa powder

**Instructions:**
1. Preheat the oven to 350F.
2. Place the pastry shells on a lined baking sheet and bake for 12-15 minutes, or until golden.
3. In a medium-sized bowl, combine the cream and chocolate chips. Microwave in 30-second intervals, stirring between each one, until the chocolate is melted and smooth.
4. Once the pastry shells have finished baking, let cool for 15 minutes.
5. Using a spatula, spread the chocolate mixture evenly into the shells, making sure to cover the entire surface.
6. Sprinkle with cocoa powder and refrigerate for 45 minutes.
7. Serve chilled and enjoy!

**Nutrition Information**:
Calories: 330, Fat: 15g, Carbohydrates: 44g, Protein: 4g.

## 41. Raspberry-Vanilla Danish Pastries

A decadent pastry filled with sweet creamy raspberry-vanilla custard, Raspberry-Vanilla Danish Pastries are sure to be the delight of any tea party or brunch. Serve eight to ten people, and prepare in about 20 minutes with a total time of about 25 minutes.

Serving: 8 – 10 people
| Preparation Time: 20 minutes
| Ready Time: 25 minutes

**Ingredients:**
- 1/2 cup raspberry preserves
- 1/4 cup light brown sugar
- 2 teaspoons all-purpose flour
- 2 teaspoons cornstarch
- 1 teaspoon almond extract
- 2 tablespoons orange juice
- 2 teaspoons pure vanilla extract
- 1/2 cup heavy cream
- 1/2 cup milk
- 2 8- or 9-inch rounds of thawed frozen puff pastry

**Instructions:**
1. Preheat oven to 375F.
2. In a medium bowl, combine preserves, brown sugar, flour, cornstarch, almond extract, orange juice, and vanilla extract.
3. In a separate bowl, whisk together the cream and milk.
4. Cut each puff pastry round into 8 even triangles. Place the puff pastry triangles on a baking sheet lined with parchment paper.
5. Working with one triangle at a time, spoon about 1 tablespoon of the raspberry-vanilla mixture into the center of each triangle. Gently fold the outer edges up and over the raspberry-vanilla mixture. Do not cover the mixture completely.
6. Brush the pastry with the cream and milk mixture.
7. Bake for 15-20 minutes until the pastries are golden brown.

**Nutrition Information:**
Calories: 238
Carbohydrates: 32 grams
Protein: 2 grams

Fat: 12 grams
Saturated Fat: 5 grams
Sodium: 78 milligrams
Fiber: 1 gram

## 42. Orange-Marmalade Danish Pastries

These delectable Orange-Marmalade Danish Pastries are an easy and delicious breakfast treat. Made with crumbly, buttery puff pastry, a zesty orange marmalade, and sprinkled with powdered sugar, these pastries are sure to be a hit in any kitchen.
Serving: Makes 8 Danish pastries
| Preparation Time: 10 minutes
| Ready Time: 20 minutes

**Ingredients:**
- 1/2 puff pastry sheet, thawed
- 3 tablespoons orange marmalade
- Water for brushing
- 2 tablespoons butter, melted
- 2 tablespoons white sugar
- Ground or powdered sugar for dusting

**Instructions:**
1. Preheat the oven to 400F. Line a baking sheet with parchment paper.
2. Cut the puff pastry into eight equal pieces. Place the pieces onto the parchment paper.
3. Spread 1/2 tablespoon of orange marmalade onto each piece.
4. Moisten the edges of the pastry pieces with water, and fold the top and sides of each piece inwards to form a packet.
5. Brush the tops of the pastries lightly with water and sprinkle with white sugar.
6. Bake for about 15-20 minutes, until the pastries are golden brown.
7. Let cool for a few minutes before dusting with powdered sugar.

**Nutrition Information**: per danish pastry:
calories: 158, fat: 8g, saturated fat: 4g, sodium: 114mg, carbs: 19g, fiber: 0.5g, sugar: 8.3g, protein: 2.1g.

## 43. Mocha-Hazelnut Danish Pastries

Mocha-Hazelnut Danish Pastries are a delicious combination of coffee and chocolate flavors with a hint of hazelnut. These delectable pastries are a welcome treat for breakfast, dessert, or an afternoon snack.
Serving: 8
| Preparation Time: 30 minutes
| Ready Time: 1 hour and 20 minutes

### Ingredients
- 2 sheets puff pastry, thawed
- 1/2 cup chocolate-hazelnut spread
- 2 tablespoons cream cheese
- 2 tablespoons butter, melted
- 2 tablespoons light brown sugar
- 2 tablespoons semi-sweet chocolate chips
- 1 tablespoon espresso powder
- 1/4 teaspoon ground cinnamon
- 2 tablespoons heavy cream
- 1 egg, lightly beaten

### Instructions
1. Preheat oven to 400F. Line 2 baking sheets with parchment paper.
2. On lightly floured surface, roll each puff pastry sheet into a 9x13-inch rectangle.
3. Spread 1/4 cup chocolate-hazelnut spread over each puff pastry rectangle.
4. In a small bowl, mix together cream cheese, butter, brown sugar, chocolate chips, espresso powder, and cinnamon until combined.
5. Spread cream cheese mixture over chocolate-hazelnut spread on puff pastry.
6. Cut each rectangle into 8 triangles and place 2-inches apart on prepared baking sheet.
7. Whisk together cream and egg in a small bowl. Brush egg wash over pastries.
8. Bake for 20 minutes or until puff pastry is golden brown.

**Nutrition Information**
Serving Size: 1 pastry
Calories: 290
Total Fat: 18 g
Saturated Fat: 8 g
Cholesterol: 40 mg
Sodium: 150 mg
Total Carbohydrates: 28 g
Dietary Fiber: 1 g
Sugars: 8 g
Protein: 4 g

## 44. Hazelnut-Coconut Danish Pastries

Satisfy your sweet tooth and indulge in Hazelnut-Coconut Danish Pastries. Filled with rich and creamy chocolate hazelnut spread and a coconut cream, these pastries are the perfect way to brighten up a brunch or afternoon pick-me-up snack.
Serving: 12 pastries
| Preparation Time: 40 minutes
| Ready Time: 70 minutes

**Ingredients:**
- All-purpose flour: 6 cups
- Salt: 2 teaspoons
- Sugar: 2 tablespoons
- Active dry yeast: 2 1/4 teaspoons
- Egg, lightly beaten: 1
- Cold unsalted butter, cut into small pieces: 3/4 cup
- Nutella or another chocolate hazelnut spread: 1 cup
- Coconut cream: 1 cup
- Powdered sugar for dusting

**Instruction:**
1. In a large mixing bowl, whisk or stir together the flour, salt, and sugar.
2. Create a well in the dry ingredients and add the yeast, egg, and butter. stir to combine, then knead until the dough is soft and smooth.

3. Place the dough on a lightly floured surface and roll out. Cut into 12 equal-sized rectangles.
4. Spread the Nutella on each rectangle and then place 1-2 tablespoons of the coconut cream on top.
5. Push the edges together and form into a round shape.
6. Place the prepared pastries on a parchment-lined baking sheet and bake in a preheated 350 degree oven for 25-30 minutes until golden.
7. Dust with powdered sugar and enjoy.

**Nutrition Information**: Per serving:
387 calories, 19g fat, 45g carbohydrates, 12g protein.

## 45. Chocolate-Cherry Danish Pastries

These Chocolate-Cherry Danish Pastries combine rich chocolate and creamy cheesecake filling with delicious cherry preserves. Perfect for any breakfast or brunch, they are sure to be a family favorite.
Serving: 8 to 10
| Preparation Time: 20 minutes
| Ready Time: 2 hours 15 minutes

**Ingredients:**
1. 2 ready-made puff pastry sheets
2. 2 cups cream cheese, softened
3. 4 tablespoons of granulated sugar
4. 1/4 teaspoon salt
5. 1 teaspoon almond extract
6. 2/3 cup cherry preserves
7. 1/4 cup dark chocolate chips

**Instructions:**
1. Preheat oven to 375 degrees F.
2. Unfold one of the puff pastry sheets and place on a lightly floured surface. Cut the sheet into four equal squares.
3. In a bowl, combine the cream cheese, sugar, salt, and almond extract, stirring until creamy.
4. Divide the cream cheese mixture evenly between the four pastry squares.

5. Place a tablespoon of cherry preserves on top of each square and top with a few chocolate chips.
6. Take the remaining sheet of puff pastry and cut it into four equal squares. Place one of the pastry squares on top of each of the cream cheese-filled pastry squares. Crimp the edges with a fork to seal.
7. Place on a greased baking sheet and bake for 20 minutes or until golden brown.
8. Allow to cool before serving.

**Nutrition Information**: Per Serving:
Calories: 283, Total Fat: 13.0g, Cholesterol: 36.9mg, Sodium: 172.7mg, Carbohydrates: 33.6g; Dietary Fiber: 1.6g, Sugars: 15.9g, Protein: 4.7g.

## 46. Mascarpone-Almond Danish Pastries

Mascarpone-Almond Danish Pastries are a unique and delicious pastry treat perfect for any occasion. Rich and creamy mascarpone cheese creates a fluffy center stuffed with toasted almonds, enveloped in crunchy and sweet pastry dough.
Serves 6, | Preparation Time 40 mins, ready in 1 hour.

**Ingredients:**
- 2/3 cup all-purpose flour
- 2 tablespoons butter, melted
- 2 tablespoons cold water
- 2 cups mascarpone cheese
- 1/2 teaspoon vanilla extract
- 2/3 cup toasted almonds, chopped
- 2 tablespoons granulated sugar
- 2 eggs

**Instructions:**
1. Preheat oven to 375F. Line baking sheet with parchment paper.
2. In a large bowl, combine flour, butter, and cold water to form a dough. Knead the dough 8-10 times. Wrap dough in plastic and chill for 30 minutes.
3. In a medium bowl, beat mascarpone and vanilla until combined. Add almonds and stir until incorporated.

4. Roll dough into 12-inch circle. Cut circle into 6 equal pieces and place a scoop of the almond mascarpone filling into the center of each piece. Then, fold the edges of the pastry over the cheese and pinch together.
5. Brush the top of the pastry with beaten eggs and sprinkle with sugar. Place on prepared baking sheet.
6. Bake in preheated oven for 15-20 minutes, or until nicely browned. Allow pastries to cool before serving.

**Nutrition Information:**
Serving size: 1 pastry
Calories: 244
Total Fat: 13g
Saturated Fat: 6g
Cholesterol: 72mg
Sodium: 86mg
Carbohydrates: 26g
Fiber: 1g
Sugar: 5g
Protein: 6g

## 47. Creamy Custard Filled Danish Pastries

Creamy Custard Filled Danish Pastries are a delicious yet simple breakfast or snack treat. Made from puff pastry filled with a creamy custard, these pastries are sure to please.
Serves: 8 | Preparation Time: 20 minutes | Ready Time: 1 hour

**Ingredients:**
– 1 sheet frozen puff pastry
– 1 cup custard
– 1 egg
– 1/2 teaspoon vanilla extract

**Instructions:**
1. Preheat oven to 400°F.
2. Lay out the puff pastry and slice into 8 equal portions.
3. Place the custard into a bowl and mix in an egg and the vanilla extract.
4. Place a spoonful of the custard mixture onto each pastry piece.

5. Fold the pastry into a triangle shape, then twist the edges to seal.
6. Place onto a baking sheet and brush the tops with a beaten egg.
7. Bake for 15 minutes or until golden brown.

**Nutrition Information**: per serving
 205cal, 4g fat, 29g carbs, 4g protein

## 48. Apple-Pecan Danish Pastries

Enjoy the flavorful combination of apples, pecans, and layers of sweet flaky dough with these Apple-Pecan Danish Pastries! This delectable pastry can be served as a unique breakfast treat or a decadent dessert.
Serving: Makes 12 pastries
| Preparation Time: 40 minutes
| Ready Time: 55 minutes

**Ingredients:**
- 2 tablespoons butter
- 1 Granny Smith or Honeycrisp apple, peeled, cored, and diced
- 2 tablespoons white sugar
- 1 cup pecans, chopped
- 2 tablespoons apple juice or apple cider
- 2 tablespoons all-purpose flour
- 2 premade pastry dough sheets

**Instructions:**
1. Preheat oven to 350 degrees F (175 degrees C). Grease a baking sheet.
2. Heat the butter in a medium skillet over medium heat. Add the apple, sugar, and pecans to the skillet. Saute for about 10 minutes or until apples are soft. Add the apple juice or cider; mix well and cook until liquid is absorbed. Set aside to cool.
3. Dust your work surface and the rolling pin with some all-purpose flour. Unwrap one sheet of store-bought pastry dough, and roll it out to approximately 1/8 inch thickness. Cut circles of dough using cookie cutter or glass and place onto prepared baking sheet.
4. Add a spoonful of the cooled apple mixture to the center of each pastry.

5. Roll out remaining pastry dough and cut out circles to match the first. Place the circles on top of each pastry and press the edges together with a fork.

6. Bake for 25 to 30 minutes in the preheated oven, or until edges are golden brown.

**Nutrition Information**: Per Serving:
253 calories | 13g fat | 30g carbohydrates | 2g protein.

## 49. Coconut-Lemon Danish Pastries

Coconut-Lemon Danish Pastries is a unique and delicious twist on traditional Danish pastries. Sweet, flaky, and tart, these pastries are sure to be a hit with the whole family. Making them requires some patience, but the end results are worth it.

Serving: 10
| Preparation Time: 45 minutes
| Ready Time: 1 hour and 45 minutes

**Ingredients:**
– 2 cups all-purpose flour
– 1/4 cup sugar
– 1/2 teaspoon baking powder
– 1/2 teaspoon salt
– 1/2 cup unsalted butter, chilled
– 2/3 cup coconut milk
– 1 tablespoon lemon zest
– 2 tablespoons fresh lemon juice
– 1/2 cup sweetened shredded coconut
– 2 tablespoons confectioners' sugar, for garnish

**Instructions:**
1. Preheat your oven to 375F and line a baking sheet with parchment paper.
2. In a large bowl, mix together the flour, sugar, baking powder, and salt.
3. Cut in the chilled butter and mix until the mixture resembles coarse meal.

4. Add the coconut milk, lemon zest and juice, and shredded coconut and mix until a somewhat sticky dough forms.
5. Cut the dough into 10 equal pieces.
6. Roll each piece into a ball and place on prepared baking sheet.
7. Bake for 25-30 minutes or until golden brown.
8. Once cool, garnish with confectioners' sugar.

**Nutrition Information**: per serving:
Calories: 311, Total Fat: 16g, Saturated Fat: 11g, Cholesterol: 34mg, Sodium: 142mg, Total Carbohydrate: 35g, Dietary Fiber: 2g, Protein: 3g

## 50. Chocolate-Almond Danish Pastries

Soft, flaky and utterly irresistible, Chocolate-Almond Danish Pastries are the perfect sweet treat for any occasion. These delicious pastries combine a crisp and buttery dough with a generous helping of smooth dark chocolate and crunchy, toasted almonds for a truly divine breakfast or dessert.
Serving: 12
| Preparation Time: 45 minutes
| Ready Time: 1 hour

**Ingredients:**
For the pastry:
- 2 tablespoons sugar
- Pinch of salt
- 2 cups all-purpose flour
- 12 tablespoons cold butter, cut into small cubes
- 1/4 cup ice water
For the chocolate-almond filling:
- 6 ounces semi-sweet chocolate, chopped
- 1/4 cup whole natural almonds, toasted and roughly chopped

**Instructions:**
1. To make the pastry, in a large bowl, whisk together the sugar, salt, and flour.

2. Using a pastry blender or two knives, cut the butter into the dry ingredients until the mixture looks crumbly. Add the cold water, and mix until a dough forms.
3. Turn the dough out onto a lightly floured surface and knead for 1 minute then form into a disk shape. Wrap the disk in plastic wrap and refrigerate for 30 minutes.
4. Preheat oven to 375F.
5. To make the filling, melt the chocolate in a double boiler, stirring often. Remove from heat and stir in the toasted almonds.
6. On a lightly floured surface, roll the dough out into a 12-inch circle then cut the dough into 12 wedges.
7. Place 1 teaspoon of chocolate-almond filling onto each wedge. Roll the wedges up, tucking the point of each wedge under to make a crescent shape.
8. Place the pastry onto a parchment-lined baking sheet and bake for 20 minutes, or until golden.

**Nutrition Information**:
Calories: 188; Fat: 11g; Cholesterol: 23mg; Sodium: 182mg; Carbohydrates: 17g; Protein: 3g.

## 51. Hot Chocolate Filled Danish Pastries

Hot Chocolate Filled Danish Pastries are an irresistible treat everyone will love. These luscious pastries have a flaky, buttery crust and a rich, creamy filling. The hot chocolate-filled center is sure to satisfy any sweet tooth.
Serving: 10
| Preparation Time: 25 minutes
| Ready Time: 40 minutes

**Ingredients:**
- 2 sheets of puff pastry.
- 2 tablespoons butter melted.
- 2 cups marshmallows.
- 1/4 cup dark or semi-sweet cocoa powder.
- 2 tablespoons water.
- 2 tablespoons sugar.

**Instructions:**
1. Preheat oven to 400F (200°C).
2. Cut each sheet of puff pastry into 5-inch squares. Place the squares on a parchment lined baking sheet.
3. Cut a 1-inch slit in the center of each square, leaving a 1/2-inch border around the sides.
4. In a small bowl, mix together the melted butter, marshmallows, cocoa powder, water, and sugar.
5. Spoon 1-2 tablespoons of the mixture into the center of each pastry square.
6. Fold the pastry over the filling and press the edges to seal.
7. Brush with remaining melted butter.
8. Bake for 15-20 minutes until the pastries are golden brown.
9. Allow to cool before serving.

**Nutrition Information** (per serving):
190 calories, 10g fat, 24g carbohydrates, 2g protein.

## 52. Pecan-Honey Danish Pastries

Pecan-Honey Danish Pastries are a delicious combination of crunchy pecans, honey, and light buttery pastry. Enjoy these sweet treats for breakfast, or as an afternoon snack.
Serving: 10-12
| Preparation Time: 45 minutes
| Ready Time: 2 hours

**Ingredients:**
- 2 cups all-purpose flour
- 1/2 teaspoon salt
- 2 tablespoons sugar
- 1/4 cup butter
- 2 tablespoons nonfat dry milk powder
- 1/2 cup cold water
- 2 tablespoons vegetable shortening
- 1/2 cup finely chopped pecans
- 1/4 cup honey

- 2 tablespoons butter

**Instructions:**
1. In a medium bowl, combine flour, salt and sugar. Cut in butter and dry milk powder until the mixture holds together and looks like coarse crumbs.
2. Add cold water, vegetable shortening and stir until mixture forms a ball.
3. On a lightly floured board, roll out the dough to a 12-inch circle. Place the dough on a greased baking sheet.
4. Sprinkle the chopped pecans over the dough and spread honey evenly over the pecans.
5. Cut the dough into 12 wedges. Roll up each wedge, starting at the outside corner.
6. Bake in a preheated 350 degree (175 degrees celsius) oven for 25 to 30 minutes or until golden brown. Cool on a wire rack and serve.

**Nutrition Information:**
Calories: 159, Total Fat: 8g, Cholesterol: 16mg, Sodium: 104mg, Total Carbohydrates: 19g, Protein: 2g.

## 53. Vanilla-Cranberry Danish Pastries

Enjoy the delicious combination of sweet vanilla and tart cranberry in these delicious Vanilla-Cranberry Danish Pastries! This recipe is easy to make and only takes 45 minutes from preparation to ready time.
Serving: 6-8 pastries
| Preparation Time: 15 minutes
| Ready Time: 30 minutes

**Ingredients:**
- 2 teaspoon of dry active yeast
- 1/4 cup of lukewarm milk
- 1/4 cup of white sugar
- 2 1/4 cups of all-purpose flour
- 1/2 teaspoon of salt
- 2 tbsp of melted butter
- 1 large egg

- Filling - 1/4 cup of fresh cranberries, minced
- 1/4 cup of white sugar
- 1/4 cup of softened butter
- 2 teaspoons of pure vanilla extract

**Instructions:**
1. In a large bowl, mix the yeast, milk, and 1/4 cup of sugar. Stir until the yeast is dissolved.
2. In a separate bowl, combine the flour and salt. Then add the melted butter, egg and yeast mixture. Mix into a ball of dough.
3. Transfer the dough to a floured work surface and knead until it is smooth. Place the dough in a lightly oiled bowl, cover with a damp cloth, and allow it to rise until doubled in size.
4. Once risen, transfer the dough to the floured work surface. Roll it out until it is about 1/4-inch thick. Cut out 6-8 circles of dough with a biscuit cutter.
5. To make the filling, beat together the softened butter, vanilla and 1/4 cup of sugar.
6. Preheat the oven to 375 degrees F. Grease a baking sheet.
7. Place each circle of dough onto the baking sheet. Spread some of the filling in the center of each circle. Top with minced cranberry.
8. Bake for 15-20 minutes, until golden brown. Let cool for about 10 minutes.

**Nutrition Information** (per serving):
Calories: 358, Fat: 17g, Protein: 4g, Carbohydrates: 46g, Cholesterol: 43mg, Sodium: 149mg, Fiber: 2g, Sugar: 9g.

## 54. Coconut-Raspberry Danish Pastries

Enjoy flavorful Coconut-Raspberry Danish Pastries for breakfast or brunch with friends and family! These flaky and buttery pastries are filled with a sweet coconut-raspberry mixture that adds just the right amount of sweetness.
Serving: Makes 12 pastries
| Preparation Time: 25 minutes
| Ready Time: 2 hours and 25 minutes

**Ingredients:**
- 2 tablespoons melted butter, cooled
- 3/4 cup all-purpose flour
- 2 tablespoons granulated sugar
- 1 teaspoon baking powder
- 1/2 teaspoon salt
- 2/3 cup coconut flakes
- 1/2 cup raspberry jam
- 1/2 cup half-and-half
- 3 tablespoons powdered sugar

**Instructions:**
1. Preheat oven to 375F. Grease a baking sheet with the melted butter and set aside.
2. In a medium bowl, whisk together the flour, sugar, baking powder and salt. Stir in the coconut flakes.
3. Add the half-and-half to the dry ingredients and stir until combined.
4. On a lightly floured surface, roll the dough into an 1/4-inch-thick rectangle. Cut the dough into 12 pieces and transfer to the prepared baking sheet.
5. Spread raspberry jam on each piece of dough.
6. Bake for 20-25 minutes, or until golden-brown. Let cool on a wire rack.
7. Dust the cooled pastries with powdered sugar and serve.

**Nutrition Information:**
Each pastry contains approximately 250 calories, 11g fat, 32g carbohydrates, 3g protein.

## 55. Cherry-Chocolate Danish Pastries

This decadent cherry-chocolate danish pastry recipe is sure to be one for the books, with its light and flaky exterior and gooey cherry-chocolate center. Everyone will love this impressive pastry and beg for seconds!
Serving: Makes 8 pastries
| Preparation Time: 45 minutes
| Ready Time: 1 hour

**Ingredients:**
-1 package of puff pastry dough
-1/2 cup cherry all-fruit spread
-1/2 cup semi-sweet chocolate chips
-1 large egg, beaten

**Instructions:**
1. Preheat oven to 375 degrees F.
2. Unroll puff pastry sheet onto lightly floured surface. Cut sheet into 8 equal pieces.
3. Place cherry all-fruit spread onto half of the puff pastry pieces and spread to the edges. In a small bowl, mix together chocolate chips and 1/4 cup of warm water and stir until smooth. Divide this mixture among the remaining puff pastry pieces.
4. Place a piece of pastry with chocolate on top of each piece with cherry, carefully pressing down to seal edges. Using a fork or a knife, crimp edges together.
5. Brush beaten egg over the top of each pastry. Place on a baking sheet lined with parchment paper and bake for 25 minutes or until golden and crisp.

**Nutrition Information** (per pastry):
210 calories, 8g fat, 29g carbohydrates, 2g protein.

## 56. Banana-Nutella Danish Pastries

This delicious sweet treat combines the classic flavors of bananas and Nutella with flaky, buttery Danish pastry. These Banana-Nutella Danish Pastries will delight your taste buds and reward you with an indulgent and satisfyingly sweet flavor.
Serving: 8-10 Danish pastries
| Preparation Time: 25 minutes
| Ready Time: 60 minutes

**Ingredients:**
- 1 sheet puff pastry
- 2 small bananas, peeled and mashed
- Nutella

- 2 tablespoons granulated sugar
- 2 tablespoons butter, melted

**Instructions:**
1. Preheat oven to 400 degrees Fahrenheit.
2. On lightly floured surface, roll out puff pastry and evenly spread mashed bananas on top, leaving a 1/2 inch margin around edges.
3. Spread Nutella into an even layer over mashed bananas. Sprinkle sugar over the entire surface.
4. Roll up the puff pastry jelly-roll style, beginning from the longest side. Cut into 2 -inch slices and place them on a parchment-lined baking sheet.
5. Brush melted butter over the slices and bake for 20-25 minutes, or until golden brown. Let cool before serving.

**Nutrition Information**:
Calories: 213, Fat: 8.8 g, Cholesterol: 10.5 mg, Sodium: 112.2 mg, Carbs: 27.9 g, Protein: 2.6 g

## 57. Hazelnut-Mocha Danish Pastries

Treat yourself to a gourmet breakfast with these delicious Hazelnut-Mocha Danish Pastries. With warm hazelnut spread, sweet mocha filling, and a light, flaky pastry base, these pastries are sure to brighten up any morning.
Serving: Makes 8 large pastries
| Preparation Time: 30 minutes
| Ready Time: 2 hours

**Ingredients**
For the Pastry:
1. 2 1/2 cups all-purpose flour
2. 3/4 teaspoon salt
3. 3 sticks (12 ounces) unsalted butter, cold, cut into small cubes
4. 1/3 cup plus 2 tablespoons cold water

For the Hazelnut-Mocha Filling:
1. 1/2 cup hazelnut spread
2. 3 tablespoons strong coffee
3. 2 tablespoons cocoa powder

4. 2 tablespoons light corn syrup

**Instructions:**
1. Make the Pastry: In a large bowl, combine the flour and salt. Add the butter cubes and mix with a pastry blender or two forks, until the butter is in pea-sized pieces. Sprinkle the cold water over the mixture, one tablespoon at a time, stirring lightly. Gather up the pastry dough and shape it into a 5-inch disk. Wrap it securely in plastic wrap and refrigerate for 1 hour.
2. Preheat the oven to 375F. Grease a large sheet pan.
3. Assemble the Pastries: On a lightly floured surface, roll out the pastry dough into a rectangle about 12 x 16 inches. Cut the rectangle into 8 equal squares. Place the squares on the prepared sheet pan.
4. Make the Hazelnut-Mocha Filling: In a medium bowl, combine the hazelnut spread, coffee, cocoa, and corn syrup. Mix until everything is well combined.
5. Assemble the Pastries: Place about 2 teaspoons of the filling into the center of the each square. Overlap opposite corners of the dough over the filling, pressing down the edges.
6. Bake the Pastries: Bake for 25-30 minutes, or until the pastries are golden brown. Allow to cool before serving.

**Nutrition Information:**
Per Serving: 1190 calories; 78g fat; 83g carbohydrates; 21g protein; 15g fiber; 281mg sodium

## 58. Apricot-Chocolate Danish Pastries

Sweet and tart, Apricot-Chocolate Danish Pastries are a simple yet delicious sweet treat that is sure to please any crowd. Utilizing two iconic flavors, this recipe pairs fragrant apricot jam with creamy milk chocolate for the ultimate bite of indulgence.
Serving: 8 pastries
| Preparation Time: 25 minutes
| Ready Time: 45 minutes

**Ingredients:**
1. 2 cups all-purpose flour

2. 2 tablespoons confectioners' sugar
3. 1/2 teaspoon salt
4. 2/3 cup cold unsalted butter
5. 1/3 cup cold water
6. 1 egg
7. 3 tablespoons apricot jam
8. 3 ounces milk chocolate, chopped

**Instructions:**
1. Combine the flour, confectioners' sugar, and salt in a food processor. Cut the cold butter into small cubes and add to the food processor. Pulse the food processor until the mixture resembles coarse meal.
2. Slowly add the cold water until the mixture forms a cohesive ball. Wrap the dough in plastic wrap and chill for at least 30 minutes.
3. Preheat oven to 375 degrees. Line a baking sheet with parchment paper.
4. On a lightly floured surface, roll the dough into a 12" x 8" rectangle. Cut the dough into 8, 3" square pieces. Place on the prepared baking sheet.
5. Beat the egg and brush the tops of the pastries with the egg mixture. Place 1/2 teaspoon of apricot jam in the center of each pastry. Sprinkle with chopped chocolate and press down lightly.
6. Bake for 15 minutes, or until golden and bubbly. Cool before serving.

**Nutrition Information**: Per pastry:
344 calories, 19g fat, 38g carbohydrates, 7g protein

## 59. Coffee-Cinnamon Danish Pastries

Coffee-Cinnamon Danish Pastries are a delicious, indulgent treat for brunch or dessert. Combining the rich flavors of espresso and cinnamon, these pastries are sure to be a hit with guests of all ages.
Serving: 12 pastries
| Preparation Time: 15 minutes
| Ready Time: 45 minutes

**Ingredients:**
- 1 sheet puff pastry, thawed

- 4 teaspoons of instant espresso powder
- 2 teaspoons ground cinnamon
- 3 Tablespoons of brown sugar
- 12 teaspoon honey
- 1 egg, beaten

**Instructions:**
1. Preheat oven to 400 degrees F.
2. On a lightly floured surface, roll out puff pastry to a 10x12-inch rectangle.
3. In a small bowl, mix together espresso powder, cinnamon, and brown sugar.
4. Sprinkle the espresso-cinnamon mixture evenly over the puff pastry.
5. Starting at one long side, roll up dough into a log.
6. Cut log into 12 slices and place on a baking sheet.
7. Brush each slice with beaten egg and a teaspoon of honey.
8. Bake for approximately 15-20 minutes until golden brown.

**Nutrition Information:**
Serving size: 1 pastry
Calories: 181, Total Fat: 8 grams, Sodium: 195 mg, Total Carbohydrates: 24 grams, Sugars: 5 grams, Protein: 2.5 grams

## 60. Orange-Whiskey Danish Pastries

This easy Orange-Whiskey Danish Pastry recipe is a delicious breakfast treat that is sure to satisfy all of your cravings. It is a flaky pastry filled with orange zest and whiskey glaze that is sure to impress.
Serving: 8
| Preparation Time: 30 minutes
| Ready Time: 1 hour

**Ingredients:**
- 4 cups all-purpose flour
- 1/2 teaspoon salt
- 1 teaspoon baking powder
- 2/3 cup cold butter, cubed
- 1 cup milk

- 1/2 cup orange juice
- 2 tablespoons orange zest
- 1 teaspoon ground cinnamon
- 1/2 cup granulated sugar
- 1 cup whiskey-flavored liqueur
- 3 tablespoons powdered sugar

**Instructions:**
1. Preheat the oven to 375 degrees F. Grease an 8-inch square baking dish.
2. In a large bowl, whisk together the flour, salt and baking powder. Cut in the cold butter cubes with a pastry blender or two knives until the mixture resembles coarse meal.
3. In another bowl, mix the milk, orange juice, orange zest, cinnamon, granulated sugar and whiskey-flavored liqueur. Add this to the flour mixture and combine completely.
4. Divide the dough in half and roll out on a lightly floured surface until it is about 1/4-inch thick. Cut into 8-inch squares.
5. Place the pastry in the prepared baking dish and sprinkle with the powdered sugar.
6. Bake for 25-30 minutes until the pastries are golden brown. Allow to cool and serve.

**Nutrition Information:**
Calories: 299, Total Fat: 8g, Saturated Fat: 5g, Cholesterol: 19mg, Sodium: 137mg, Total Carbohydrate: 47g, Dietary Fiber: 1g, Protein: 4g

## 61. Walnut-Custard Danish Pastries

Walnut-Custard Danish Pastries are a wonderfully decadent dessert that are sure to satisfy the sweet tooth of any eater. The flaky pastry dough is filled with a nutty, creamy walnut-custard filling and is the ultimate treat for any occasion.

Serving: 12 people
| Preparation Time: 25 minutes
| Ready Time: 1 1/2 hours

**Ingredients:**

Pastry Dough:
- 2 1/2 cups all-purpose flour
- 2 tbsp granulated sugar
- 3/4 tsp salt
- 2 sticks unsalted butter, cold and cut into small cubes
- 6-8 tbsp ice water

Walnut-Custard Filling:
- 3/4 cup walnuts, chopped
- 2 large eggs, beaten
- 1 cup whole milk
- 1 tsp vanilla extract
- 1/4 cup granulated sugar
- 3 1/2 tbsp all-purpose flour
- 2 tbsp unsalted butter, melted

**Instructions:**
1. In a medium size bowl, whisk together the flour, sugar, and salt.
2. Cut in the butter with a pastry blender until the butter pieces look like small peas.
3. Gradually add the ice water, one tablespoon at a time until the dough forms a ball.
4. Wrap the dough in plastic wrap and refrigerate for at least one hour.
5. Preheat oven to 375F.
6. To make the walnut-custard filling, combine the walnuts, eggs, milk, vanilla, sugar, flour, and butter in a medium-large bowl; stir to combine.
7. On a lightly floured surface, roll the dough out to 1/4 inch thick.
8. Cut the dough into 12 round circles (using a biscuit cutter or a glass tumbler).
9. Place a spoonful of the walnut-custard mixture into the center of each round.
10. Pinch the edges of the dough together to seal the filling inside.
11. Place the pastries on a parchment lined baking sheet and bake until golden brown and crispy, about 20-25 minutes.
12. Allow to cool before serving.

**Nutrition Information** (Per Serving):
Calories: 313 · Total Fat: 16.5 g · Sodium: 206 mg · Total Carbs: 33.8 g · Sugars: 6.4 g · Protein: 6.1 g

## 62. Pecan-White Chocolate Danish Pastries

This delectable Pecan-White Chocolate Danish Pastries recipe is an easy-to-make pastry that is perfect for a special breakfast or dessert. This sweet pastry is a combination of white chocolate, pecans, and a buttery croissant dough, layered and baked until golden brown. Serve this pastry for a special occasion or treat your family and friends to a luxurious breakfast.

Serving: 12
| Preparation Time: 15-20 minutes
| Ready Time: 20 minutes

**Ingredients:**
1. 1 (8 ounce) package refrigerated crescent rolls
2. 2 tablespoons butter, melted
3. 2/3 cup white chocolate chips
4. 1/3 cup chopped pecans
5. 1/2 teaspoon ground cinnamon
6. 1 tablespoon granulated sugar

**Instructions:**
1. Preheat oven to 375F. Grease a 9-inch round cake pan and set aside.
2. Unroll crescent rolls and press into the bottom of the prepared pan. Brush the melted butter over the dough.
3. Sprinkle the white chocolate chips and pecans evenly over the top of the dough. Sprinkle the top with cinnamon and sugar.
4. Bake in preheated oven for 15-20 minutes, or until the top is golden brown.

**Nutrition Information:**
Calories per serving: 320, Fat: 21g, Cholesterol: 7mg, Sodium: 265mg, Carbohydrates: 28g, Protein: 4g.

## 63. Almond-Coconut Danish Pastries

Almond-Coconut Danish Pastries is a mouth watering and sweet treat that will tantalize the taste buds. These flakey pastries are a great addition

to any breakfast or brunch and can be made ahead of time and enjoyed all week.
Serving: 8
| Preparation Time: 20 minutes.
| Ready Time: 40 minutes.

**Ingredients:**
- 1 (8 ounce) package crescent roll dough
- 1/3 cup almond paste
- 1/2 cup sweetened flaked coconut
- 2 tablespoons butter, melted
- 2 tablespoons sugar

**Instructions:**
1. Preheat oven to 350 degrees F (175 degrees C).
2. Unroll and separate the crescent roll dough, pinching the seams together.
3. Divide the almond paste into 8 equal pieces and place over dough.
4. Sprinkle with coconut, butter, and sugar.
5. Roll up, starting with the wider end.
6. Place on a greased baking sheet, seam-side down.
7. Bake for 25 to 30 minutes, until golden brown.

**Nutrition Information:**
Calories: 185
Total Fat: 10g
Saturated Fat: 5g
Cholesterol: 15mg
Sodium: 225mg
Total Carbohydrates: 20g
Protein: 2g

## 64. Cranberry-Cream Cheese Danish Pastries

Enjoy a decadent pastry that features the sweet and tart combination of cranberries and cream cheese swirled together in a delightfully flaky Danish. These Cranberry-Cream Cheese Danish Pastries make for a delicious afternoon snack or breakfast treat!

Serving: Makes 18-22 Danish pastries
| Preparation Time: 35 minutes
| Ready Time: 1 hour, 20 minutes

**Ingredients:**
-Plain white flour – 2 1/4 cups
-Milk – 1/2 cup
-Egg – 1
-Salt – 1 teaspoon
-Butter – 3 tablespoons
-Cream cheese – 3 ounces
-Granulated sugar – 1/2 cup
-Dried cranberries – 1/2 cup

**Instructions:**
1. Preheat the oven to 190°C / 375F.
2. In a medium bowl, mix the milk, egg, salt, butter, and plain white flour. Knead the dough until it forms a soft and pliable ball. Then set it aside to rest while you prepare the filling.
3. In another bowl, mix the cream cheese, sugar, and dried cranberries until you create an even, thick mixture.
4. Cut the dough into 18-22 equal-sized pieces (depending on serving size).
5. Take each piece of dough and roll into an oval shape. Place 1-2 tablespoons of the cream cheese mixture onto the center of the oval.
6. Bring one edge of the oval up and over the filling. Then bring the other edge up and over, pressing to seal the edges.
7. Place the Danish pastries onto a greased, parchment-lined baking sheet and bake for 20 minutes at 190°C / 375F.

**Nutrition Information:** Per serving (1 Danish pastry):
-Calories: 208
-Total Fat: 9.7g
-Saturated Fat: 6.2g
-Carbohydrates: 23.7g
-Protein: 5.2g

## 65. Maple-Pecan Danish Pastries

A mouth-watering combination of sweet maple syrup and crunchy pecans, this Maple-Pecan Danish Pastry is a perfect treat for any gathering.
Serving: Makes 30 pastries.
| Preparation Time: 20 minutes
| Ready Time: 1 hour

**Ingredients:**
- 2 tablespoons melted butter
- 2 eggs
- 1/2 cup maple syrup
- 1 cup heavy cream
- 2 1/2 cups all-purpose flour
- 1 teaspoon baking powder
- 1/2 teaspoon salt
- 2 cups chopped pecans

**Instructions:**
1. Preheat oven to 375F.
2. In a large bowl, mix together the butter, eggs, maple syrup and heavy cream.
3. In a separate bowl, sift together the flour, baking powder and salt.
4. Add the dry ingredients to the wet ingredients and mix until a dough forms.
5. Stir in the chopped pecans.
6. On a floured surface, roll out the dough to about 1/4 inch thickness.
7. Cut the dough into 2-inch squares and place onto a parchment-lined baking sheet.
8. Bake for 15-20 minutes or until the pastries are golden brown.
9. Let cool before serving.

**Nutrition Information**:
Serving Size 1 pastrie; Calories: 160; Total Fat: 8g; Saturated Fat: 3g; Cholesterol: 16mg; Sodium: 78 mg; Total Carbohydrate: 19g; Fiber: 2g; Sugars: 5g; Protein: 3g.

## 66. Pumpkin-Cinnamon Danish Pastries

A sweet pumpkin treat, these Pumpkin-Cinnamon Danish Pastries are a delicious blend of cinnamon, pumpkin, and cream cheese. Serve them for dessert or breakfast with coffee or tea.
Serving: 8-10
| Preparation Time: 30 minutes
| Ready Time: 1 hour

**Ingredients:**
- 2 cups all-purpose flour
- 2 tablespoons sugar
- 2 teaspoons baking powder
- 1/2 teaspoon baking soda
- 1/4 teaspoon salt
- 1/4 cup butter, chilled and cubed
- 2 tablespoons vegetable shortening, chilled and cubed
- 3/4 cup canned pumpkin puree
- 2 large eggs
- 2 tablespoons milk
- 1 teaspoon ground cinnamon
- 1/4 teaspoon ground nutmeg
- 1 (8-ounce) package cream cheese, softened
- 2/3 cup confectioners' sugar

**Instructions:**
1. Preheat oven to 375 degrees F (190 degrees C). Grease one baking sheet.
2. In a medium bowl, mix together the flour, sugar, baking powder, baking soda, and salt. Cut in the butter and shortening until the mixture resembles coarse crumbs.
3. In a separate bowl, beat together the pumpkin, eggs, milk, cinnamon, and nutmeg. Stir in the flour mixture until just moistened.
4. On a lightly floured surface, roll the dough out to 1/8-inch thickness. Cut into circles using a 3-inch biscuit cutter. Place circles on the prepared cookie sheet.
5. Bake for 10 minutes in the preheated oven.
6. Meanwhile, beat together the cream cheese and confectioners' sugar until creamy. Pipe a circle of the cream cheese mixture onto each pastry.

7. Bake for an additional 10 minutes in the preheated oven, or until pastries are golden brown. Cool before serving.

**Nutrition Information**:
Per serving (serving size: 1 pastry): 210 calories; 12.2 g fat; 18.6 g carbohydrates; 3.9 g protein

## 67. Caramel-Pumpkin Danish Pastries

These Caramel-Pumpkin Danish Pastries are an indulgent filled breakfast treat. They're made with sweet caramel and spiced pumpkin for a breakfast experience that is sure to please.
Serving: 6-8
| Preparation Time: 10 minutes
| Ready Time: 1 hour

**Ingredients:**
1. 2 sheets puff pastry, thawed
2. 2 cups pumpkin puree
3. 3/4 cup brown sugar
4. 1/2 teaspoon ground cinnamon
5. 1/4 teaspoon sea salt
6. 1/4 teaspoon grated nutmeg
7. 3/4 cup caramel sauce

**Instructions:**
1. Preheat the oven to 400 degrees F. Line two baking sheets with parchment paper.
2. On a lightly floured surface, roll out each sheet of puff pastry. Cut out 12 3-inch circles with a biscuit or cookie cutter. Place the circles onto the lined baking sheets.
3. In a medium bowl, mix together the pumpkin puree, brown sugar, ground cinnamon, sea salt and nutmeg.
4. Place 1 tablespoon of the pumpkin filling in the center of each pastry circle. Top with 1 teaspoon of the caramel sauce.
5. Fold the edges of the puff pastry up and around the filling, creating a small bowl. Crimp the edges together to seal. Bake for 15-20 minutes or until golden brown.

**Nutrition Information**:
Calories: 200, Total Fat: 10 g, Saturated Fat: 4 g, Cholesterol: 0 mg, Sodium: 120 mg, Carbohydrates: 24 g, Fiber: 2 g, Protein: 3 g.

## 68. Toffee-Chocolate Danish Pastries

Toffee-Chocolate Danish Pastries are sweet and indulgent breakfast pastries that make a delicious treat. With a flaky, buttery dough that is topped with sweet toffee and creamy chocolate chips, they offer the perfect balance of crunch and sweetness.
Serves 12. | Preparation Time 15 minutes. Ready in 40 minutes.

**Ingredients:**
- 2 packages of pre-made puff pastry (2 sheets each)
- 2 tablespoons of melted butter
- 1 tablespoon of caster sugar
- 1 teaspoon of vanilla extract
- 1 cup of toffee pieces
- 1/4 cup of chocolate chips

**Instructions:**
1. Preheat oven to 375F.
2. In a bowl, mix together melted butter, sugar, and vanilla extract.
3. Unroll the puff pastry on a lightly floured surface.
4. Brush the tops of the puff pastry with the butter mixture.
5. Sprinkle toffee pieces and chocolate chips on top.
6. Roll up the puff pastry and cut into 12 slices.
7. Place on a greased baking sheet.
8. Bake for 25 minutes.

**Nutrition Information**:
Calories: 192 per serving, Fat: 11g, Saturated Fat: 6g, Cholesterol: 4mg, Sodium: 119mg, Carbohydrates: 19g, Fiber: 1g, Sugar: 2g, Protein: 1g.

## 69. White Chocolate-Almond Danish Pastries

White Chocolate-Almond Danish Pastries is a delightful combination of subtle sweetness, crunchy almonds, and melt-in-your-mouth white chocolate. A perfect holiday dessert that can easily be prepared in advance, these pastries are sure to be a hit with everyone.
Serving: 12
| Preparation Time: 40 minutes
| Ready Time: 2 hours 10 minutes

**Ingredients:**
- 1/2 lb. puff pastry, thawed
-1/2 cup almond paste
-2 tablespoons white sugar
-3 tablespoons sliced almonds
-1/3 cup white chocolate chips
-1 egg white
-1 tablespoon water

**Instructions:**
1. Preheat oven to 400 degrees F (200 degrees C). Line a baking sheet with parchment paper.
2. Cut puff pastry into 12 even squares or triangles.
3. In a small bowl, mix almond paste, sugar and almonds until fully combined.
4. Place 1 teaspoon of almond paste mixture on each piece of puff pastry; spread evenly. Top with white chocolate chips.
5. In a separate small bowl, whisk egg white and water until well blended. Brush over each pastry.
6. Bake for 20 minutes, or until golden brown.

**Nutrition Information** (per serving):
Calories: 193, Fat: 12g, Cholesterol: 0mg, Sodium: 11mg, Carbohydrates: 19g, Fiber: 1g, Sugar: 5g, Protein: 4g

## 70. Matcha Powder-Coconut Danish Pastries

This Matcha Powder-Coconut Danish Pastries recipe is a combination of sweet, savory, and creamy flavors. They're fluffy, buttery, and perfect for enjoying any time of day. For added texture and a hint of coconut, a generous sprinkling of shredded coconut is added to the dough. They turn out amazing fresh out of the oven and can be stored in an airtight container for up to three days.

Serving: Makes 12 Danish pastries
| Preparation Time: 45 minutes
| Ready Time: 1 hour

**Ingredients:**
- 2/3 cup of warm milk (110 degrees Fahrenheit)
- 2/3 cup of unsalted butter, melted
- 2 1/4 teaspoon of active dry yeast
- 3 tablespoons of light-brown sugar
- 2 large eggs
- 4 cups of all-purpose flour
- 2 teaspoons of salt
- 2 tablespoons of matcha powder
- 2/3 cup of sweetened shredded coconut

**Instructions:**
1. Preheat oven to 350 degrees Fahrenheit.
2. In a mixing bowl, combine the warm milk, melted butter, stretch and sprinkle yeast, and brown sugar. Allow to sit for 5 minutes until the yeast activates and starts to bubble.
3. Whisk in the eggs until well combined, then add in the all-purpose flour, salt and matcha powder. Knead the dough until it is soft and elastic, then sprinkle in the coconut.
4. Roll out the dough onto a lightly floured surface and cut out 12 four-inch circles. Place the circles onto a parchment-lined baking sheet and bake for 20-25 minutes or until golden brown.

**Nutrition Facts:**
Per serving (1 Danish pastry), Calories 257, Fat 9.2g, Carbs 38.2g, Protein 4.6g, Cholesterol 27mg, Sodium 199mg, Sugar 5.8g.

## 71. Peanut Butter-Chocolate Danish Pastries

Enjoy a tantalizing mix of sweet chocolate and nutty peanut butter with these deliciously soft, fluffy danishes. These pastries are a great treat for special occasions, brunch, or simply indulging a craving.
Serving: 18 pieces
| Preparation Time: 30 minutes
| Ready Time: 1 hour 30 minutes

**Ingredients:**
- 2 cans (8 ounces each) refrigerated crescent rolls
- 3/4 cup peanut butter
- 1/2 cup semi-sweet chocolate chips
- 4 tablespoons butter, melted
- 2 tablespoons granulated sugar
- 1 teaspoon ground cinnamon
- Powdered sugar (optional)

**Instructions:**
1. Preheat the oven to 375F. Line a baking sheet with parchment paper.
2. Unroll the crescent roll dough and separate into 16 triangles. Place on the baking sheet.
3. In a bowl, combine the peanut butter, chocolate chips, melted butter, sugar and cinnamon.
4. Spread about 1 tablespoon of the peanut butter mixture onto the wide end of each dough triangle, reserving 2 tablespoons of the mixture.
5. Fold dough over the peanut butter mixture and roll up, starting from the wide end.
6. Place the danishes on the prepared baking sheet. Brush the remaining peanut butter mixture over the tops of the danishes.
7. Bake in preheated oven for 15-20 minutes or until golden brown.
8. Dust with powdered sugar and serve warm.

**Nutrition Information** (per serving):
210 Calories, 12g Fat, 22g Carbs, 2g Fiber, 2g Protein

## 72. Nutella-Coconut Danish Pastries

Luscious Nutella-Coconut Danish Pastries – a flaky pastry dough filled with creamy, delicious Nutella and topped with toasted coconut flakes

for an extra burst of flavor! Serve for breakfast or as a special weekend treat.
Serving: Makes 10 pastries
| Preparation Time: 30 minutes
| Ready Time: 60 minutes

**Ingredients:**
-1 can refrigerated crescent rolls
-1/2 cup Nutella
-1/4 cup toasted coconut flakes
-1/4 cup powdered sugar
-2 tablespoons melted butter

**Instructions:**
1. Preheat oven to 350°F
2. Unroll the crescent rolls, and carefully separate them and press the seams together to form one sheet of dough.
3. Cut the sheet into 10 rectangles.
4. Spread Nutella onto each rectangle, leaving a 1/2 inch border around the edges.
5. Fold up both sides of the rectangles, forming a pocket around the edges of the Nutella.
6. Sprinkle toasted coconut flakes over top.
7. Bake for 20-25 minutes, or until the pastries are lightly browned.
8. Let cool for 10 minutes before sprinkling with powdered sugar.
9. Drizzle melted butter over top.

**Nutrition Information:**
Calories: 140 per pastry, Total fat: 7g, Saturated fat: 3.3g, Cholesterol: 10mg, Sodium: 190mg, Total carbohydrates: 17g, Protein: 1.1g

## 73. Cranberry-Blueberry Danish Pastries

Impress family and friends with this delicious Cranberry-Blueberry Danish Pastries recipe. Combining sweet and tart cranberries with juicy blueberries, this recipe will make for a delightful breakfast for the whole family.
Servings: Makes 12 Pastries

| Preparation Time: 20 minutes
| Ready Time: 40 minutes

**Ingredients:**
1. 2 cans (8 oz each) refrigerated crescent rolls
2. 3/4 cups fresh cranberries
3. 2/3 cup blueberries
4. 1/2 cup sugar
5. 1/2 teaspoon ground cinnamon

**Instructions:**
1. Preheat oven to 375F. Line a baking sheet with parchment paper.
2. Unroll crescent roll dough and separate into 2 long rectangles. Place rectangles on the baking sheet and press the perforations to seal.
3. In a small bowl combine cranberries, blueberries, sugar, and cinnamon. Sprinkle the cranberry-blueberry mixture onto the crescent dough.
4. Fold the sides of the dough over the mix and use a rolling pin to seal. Cut the dough into 12 even pieces.
5. Bake for 20-25 minutes or until golden brown.

**Nutrition Information:**
Calories: 202; Total Fat: 9.7g ; Saturated Fat: 3.4g; Cholesterol: 8mg; Sodium: 247mg; Carbohydrates: 25.8g; Fiber: 1g; Protein: 1.9g

## 74. Spiced Apple-Cinnamon Danish Pastries

Spiced Apple-Cinnamon Danish Pastries are a delicious morning treat that is easy and enjoyable to make. These pastries have a light and tender texture, and are filled with sweet and spicy apples and cinnamon. Enjoy these delicacies straight out of the oven, or with a spoonful of vanilla ice cream.
Serving: 12-14 pastries
| Preparation Time: 45-50 minutes
| Ready Time: 1 hour

**Ingredients:**
1. 1 package (2 sheets) frozen puff pastry, thawed

2. 4-5 apples, peeled and chopped
3. 2-3 tablespoons brown sugar
4. 2-3 teaspoons cinnamon
5. 1 teaspoon ground nutmeg
6. 1/4 teaspoon ground cloves
7. 1 tablespoon butter, melted

**Instructions:**
1. Preheat the oven to 375 degrees Fahrenheit.
2. Unfold each sheet of puff pastry onto a lightly floured surface. With a rolling pin, roll out each sheet until it is about 1/8 inch thick.
3. In a medium bowl, mix together the chopped apples, brown sugar, cinnamon, nutmeg, and cloves.
4. Place one sheet of puff pastry onto a greased baking sheet. Spread the apple mixture over the pastry, leaving a 1-inch border. Brush the melted butter onto the edges of the dough.
5. Place the second sheet of puff pastry over the top of the first, and press the edges together to seal.
6. Cut the pastry into 12-14 triangles, and then gently stretch each triangle to form the shape of a Danish pastry.
7. Bake for 25-30 minutes, or until the pastries are golden-brown. Allow to cool for 10 minutes before serving.

**Nutrition Information:**
Calories: 181 kcal, Carbohydrates: 29 g, Protein: 3 g, Fat: 8 g, Saturated Fat: 3 g, Cholesterol: 3 mg, Sodium: 129 mg, Potassium: 108 mg, Fiber: 2 g, Sugar: 12 g, Vitamin A: 11 IU, Vitamin C: 2 mg, Calcium: 16 mg, Iron: 1 mg

## 75. Caramel-Apple Danish Pastries

Caramel-Apple Danish Pastries are a delicious twist on traditional Danish pastry. Combining a sweet apple and caramel filling with a light and flaky pastry crust, this delicious breakfast pastry is sure to please.
Servings: 24 | Preparation Time: 10 minutes | Ready Time: 25 minutes

**Ingredients:**
- 1 package pre-made puff pastry

- 2 apples, peeled, cored and diced
- 1/2 cup brown sugar
- 1/4 cup butter
- 2 tablespoons cornstarch
- 2 tablespoons cold water
- Juice of 1/2 lemon
- 1 cup caramel topping

**Instructions:**
1. Preheat oven to 400 degrees F.
2. Place puff pastry onto a lightly floured surface, cutting into 6 equal portions. Place each portion onto a parchment paper lined baking sheet.
3. In a small saucepan, melt butter over medium heat. Add apples, brown sugar, cornstarch and water. Simmer until mixture has thickened, about 5 minutes. Remove from heat and stir in lemon juice.
4. Divide apple mixture among the puff pastry portions, spooning into center of each. Top with caramel topping.
5. Bake for 13-15 minutes, or until pastry is golden brown and filling is bubbly.

**Nutrition Information**: Per Serving:
Calories: 214, Total Fat: 10.3g, Saturated Fat: 5.3g, Cholesterol: 8mg, Sodium: 153mg, Carbohydrates: 28.3g, Fiber: 1.6g, Sugar: 5.9g, Protein: 2.2g.


## 76. Chocolate-Mint Danish Pastries

Chocolate-Mint Danish Pastries are a delicious and decadent fusion of sweet and creamy flavors, perfect for the ultimate breakfast or brunch treat. A delicious blend of dark chocolate and subtle mint flavor, these pastries are sure to be a crowd pleaser.
Serving: 10 pastries
| Preparation Time: 45 minutes
| Ready Time: 2 hours

**Ingredients:**
- 1/2 cup butter
- 3/4 cup white sugar

- 1 1/2 cups all-purpose flour
- 3/4 teaspoon baking powder
- 1/4 teaspoon salt
- 1 teaspoon vanilla extract
- 1 egg
- 1/2 cup dark chocolate chips
- 1 tablespoon mint extract

**Instructions:**
1. Preheat oven to 375F. Grease a baking sheet with butter.
2. In a large bowl, cream together the butter and sugar until light and fluffy.
3. In a separate bowl, combine the flour, baking powder, and salt. Gradually add to the creamed mixture, stirring well.
4. Roll the dough into small balls, about 1 1/2 inches in diameter. Place on the prepared baking sheet.
5. Bake in the preheated oven for 10 to 12 minutes. Allow to cool slightly before adding the chocolate chips and mint extract.
6. Drizzle chocolate chips over top of the cooled pastries and let cool completely. Serve.

**Nutrition Information:**
Per Serving 270 calories; 14.4 g fat; 33.3 g carbohydrates; 3.2 g protein; 37 mg cholesterol; 100 mg sodium.

## 77. Coconut-Mango Danish Pastries

Coconut-Mango Danish Pastries is an iconic pastry dish made with flaky, buttery pastries filled with the sweet flavor of coconut and mango. This dish is perfect for special occasions and can be served with coffee and tea.
Serving: 8-10 people
| Preparation Time: 30 minutes
| Ready Time: 1 1/2 hours

**Ingredients:**
- 2/3 cup mango puree
- 1/3 cup sweetened coconut flakes

- 2 cups all-purpose flour
- 1 egg
- 1 teaspoon baking powder
- 1/2 teaspoon salt
- 1 cup unsalted butter, cubed
- 1/2 cup cold milk
- 1/4 cup powdered sugar

**Instructions:**
1. Preheat oven to 375F.
2. In a medium bowl, mix together mango puree and coconut flakes. Set aside.
3. In a separate bowl, whisk together flour, egg, baking powder and salt.
4. Cut in the cubed butter until the mixture looks like course crumbs.
5. Gradually stir in the cold milk and knead until the dough forms a ball.
6. Roll out dough on a floured surface until it is 1/4" thick.
7. Use a small biscuit cutter to cut out 8-10 circular shapes from the dough.
8. Place 1 tablespoon of the mango-coconut filling into the center of each dough piece.
9. Fold dough in half, and crimp the edges together.
10. Place pastries on a baking sheet and bake for 25-30 minutes.
11. Serve warm and sprinkle with powdered sugar.

**Nutrition Information:**
Calories: 248, Fat: 14.2g, Carbohydrates: 27.2g, Protein: 3.9g, Sodium: 186mg, Fiber: 1.7g.

## 78. Cranberry-Almond Danish Pastries

A delicious and indulgent dish, these Cranberry-Almond Danish Pastries are the perfect finish to any meal. Deliciously sweet and nutty, these pastries are an absolute delight.
Serving: 12
| Preparation Time: 15 minutes
| Ready Time: 1 hour and 15 minutes

**Ingredients:**

- 2 cups all-purpose flour
- 1/4 cup white sugar
- 1 teaspoon baking powder
- 1/4 teaspoon salt
- 1/2 cup cold butter, cubed
- 1 egg
- 2 tablespoons cold water
- 8 ounces cream cheese, softened
- 1/2 cup white sugar
- 2 tablespoons all-purpose flour
- 1/4 teaspoon almond extract
- 1/2 cup dried cranberries
- 1/4 cup finely chopped sliced almonds

**Instructions:**
1. Preheat oven to 350 degrees F (175 degrees C). Grease a baking sheet.
2. In a medium bowl, whisk together 2 cups flour, 1/4 cup sugar, baking powder and salt. Cut in butter until crumbly. using a fork, blend in egg and cold water.
3. Roll dough into a 14x8 inch rectangle on a lightly floured surface. Place on prepared baking sheet.
4. In a medium bowl, mix together cream cheese, 1/2 cup sugar, 2 tablespoons flour, and almond extract. Spread over dough to within 1/2 inch of edges. Sprinkle with cranberries and almonds.
5. Bake for 25 minutes in the preheated oven, until golden. Serve warm or at room temperature.

**Nutrition Information** (per serving):
Calories: 207
Total Fat: 9.4 g
Saturated Fat: 5.6 g
Cholesterol: 37 mg
Sodium: 123 mg
Potassium: 58 mg
Carbohydrates: 26.4 g
Fiber: 0.7 g
Sugar: 8.7 g
Protein: 3.7 g

# 79. Orange-Zest Danish Pastries

Orange-Zest Danish Pastries are made with a rich dough, layered with butter and filled with a sweet orange custard. The citrus aroma and flavor of the orange zest make this recipe a delicious and irresistible pasty treat.
Serving: 8 - 10
| Preparation Time: 1 hour
| Ready Time: 2 hours

**Ingredients:**
- 300g plain flour
- 200ml full-fat milk
- 55g caster sugar
- 3g salt
- 125g unsalted butter, softened
- 2 eggs
- Zest of 1 orange

For the custard
- 3 tbsp custard powder
- 30g caster sugar
- 500ml full-fat milk
- 1 orange, zested

**Instructions:**
1. Make the dough: Combine flour, sugar, and salt in a large bowl and mix.
2. Add the butter in cubes and mix.
3. Gradually add Eggs and milk.
4. Knead until you get a smooth dough.
5. Let the dough rest for 10 minutes, then roll it out to about 0.3 cm thickness.
6. Cut the dough into 14 cm circles and place them on a baking sheet.
7. Make the custard: Mix together the custard powder and sugar in a bowl.
8. Heat the milk in a pan and add the custard powder and sugar mixture.
9. Cook for a few minutes stirring continuously until simmering.
10. Remove from heat and stir in the orange zest.
11. Put the custard in the middle of each circle of dough.
12. Fold the dough in half to enclose the custard.

13. Brush each pastry with egg wash and bake in a preheated oven at 220°C for 20 minutes.
14. Allow to cool before serving.

**Nutrition Information:**
Calories: 150
Fat: 7g
Carbohydrates: 17g
Protein: 4g

## 80. Pistachio-Cream Cheese Danish Pastries

Try this delicious Pistachio-Cream Cheese Danish Pastries for your next brunch or breakfast get together. Made with delicious cream cheese, pistachios, and delicious puff pastry dough, this treat is sure to delight.
Serving: Makes 10-12 danish pastries
| Preparation Time: 15 minutes
| Ready Time: 45 minutes

**Ingredients:**
-1 (14 oz) package of puff pastry dough
-4 ounces cream cheese, softened
-2 tablespoons powdered sugar
-2 tablespoons of coarsely chopped pistachios
-1 egg, lightly beaten

**Instructions:**
1. Preheat the oven to 375 degrees.
2. Roll out one sheet of pastry dough on a lightly floured surface. Cut into 2.5 inch circles. Place circles onto a baking sheet lined with parchment paper.
3. In a small bowl, whisk together the cream cheese and powdered sugar until creamy and smooth. Divide the cream cheese between the pastry circles. Sprinkle each circle with crushed pistachios.
4. Roll out the second sheet of pastry dough and cut into 2.5 inch circles. Place a single circle of dough over top each of the pizzas. Press the edges of both circles together lightly with a fork. Brush each pasty lightly with the beaten egg.

5. Bake in the preheated oven for 30–35 minutes, or until lightly golden-brown. Allow the pastries to cool completely before serving.

**Nutrition Information**: Per serving:
181 calories; 8.5 g fat; 26.5 g carbohydrates; 3.1 g protein; 11 mg cholesterol; 212 mg sodium.

## 81. Lemon-Blueberry Danish Pastries

Lemon-Blueberry Danish Pastries are a delicious and easy-to-make breakfast treat. This recipe makes 12 pastries and takes approximately 30 minutes for preparation and 10 minutes for baking. Enjoy the perfectly tart and sweet flavors of this recipe all in one bite!
Serving: Makes 12 pastries
| Preparation Time: 30 minutes
| Ready Time: 10 minutes

**Ingredients:**
- 2 cups all-purpose flour
- 3 tablespoons sugar
- 1/2 teaspoon salt
- 4 ounces (1 stick) cold unsalted butter, cut into cubes
- 1/4 cup cold milk
- 1 large egg
- 1 teaspoon pure vanilla extract
- Zest of 1 lemon
- 3 tablespoons fresh lemon juice
- 2 cups blueberries
- 1 tablespoon water
- Milk, for brushing

**Instructions:**
1. Preheat the oven to 375F.
2. In a large bowl, whisk together the flour, sugar, and salt.
3. Using a pastry blender or two knives, cut the butter into the flour mixture until it is crumbly.
4. In a small bowl, whisk together the milk, egg, and vanilla.
5. Add the milk mixture to the flour mixture and stir until just combined.

6. On a lightly floured surface, roll out the dough to a rectangle about 1/4-inch thick.
7. Sprinkle the lemon zest and lemon juice over the dough.
8. Sprinkle blueberries over the top of the lemon juice.
9. Gently press the blueberries into the dough.
10. Starting from one end, roll the dough up like a jelly roll into a log.
11. Cut the log into 12 slices and place them on a parchment-lined baking sheet.
12. Brush the tops of the Danish pastries with milk.
13. Bake for 10-12 minutes until golden brown.

**Nutrition Information:**
Serving Size: 1 pastry
Calories: 203
Carbohydrates: 27 g
Protein: 3 g
Fat: 10 g
Fiber: 2 g
Sodium: 75 mg

## 82. Passion Fruit-Mango Danish Pastries

This delicious and sweet Passion Fruit-Mango Danish Pastries is a delightful treat for breakfast, brunch or a snack. Its light and soft pastry base topped with fresh passion fruit and mango glaze makes it equally tasty and visually appealing.
Serving: Makes 8 Danish pastries.
| Preparation Time: 25 minutes.
| Ready Time: 1 hour 10 minutes.

**Ingredients:**
1. Puff pastry, frozen: 400 g
2. Mango puree: 1/3 cup (85 mL)
3. Egg: 1
4. Passion Fruit pulp: 1/4 cup (60 mL)
5. Powdered sugar: 1/4 cup (60 g)
6. Water: 1 tablespoon (15 mL)

**Instructions:**
1. Preheat the oven to 350F (180°C / Gas Mark 5). Line a baking sheet with baking paper.
2. Place a sheet of puff pastry on a lightly floured work surface. Roll it out slightly. Cut it into 8 pieces and place them on the baking sheet.
3. In a small bowl, mix together the mango puree, egg, passion fruit pulp, sugar and water.
4. Spread the mixture evenly onto each pastry.
5. Bake in the preheated oven for 20 to 25 minutes, or until golden brown.
6. Let cool for 10 minutes before serving.

**Nutrition Information:**
Calories: 208/ serving, Total Fat: 11g, Saturated Fat: 2g, Cholesterol: 10mg, Sodium: 82mg, Potassium: 101mg, Carbohydrates: 25g, Fiber: 1g, Sugar: 11g, Protein: 3g.

## 83. Strawberry-Banana Danish Pastries

Enjoy these delightful, delicate Strawberry-Banana Danish pastries, which boast a unique combination of two of the most popular summer fruits. A perfect treat for any special occasion!
Serving: Makes 6 Danishes
| Preparation Time: 20 minutes
| Ready Time: 45 minutes

**Ingredients:**
- 2 cups all-purpose flour
- 2 tablespoons sugar
- 1/4 teaspoon salt
- 2/3 cup cold butter
- 1/2 cup cold water
- 1 egg, lightly beaten
- 1/2 cup strawberry jam
- 1 peeled and mashed banana

**Instructions:**
Step 1: Preheat the oven to 375 degrees F.

Step 2: Combine the flour, sugar, and salt in a medium-sized bowl.
Step 3: Cut in the butter until the mixture resembles a coarse meal.
Step 4: Add the water gradually to the mixture and mix until it forms a soft dough.
Step 5: Knead the dough on a lightly floured surface for 3 to 4 minutes.
Step 6: Roll the dough out to 1/2-inch thickness.
Step 7: Cut the dough into six 4-inch circles.
Step 8: Place the circles on a lightly greased baking sheet.
Step 9: Brush the edges of the circles with a bit of the beaten egg.
Step 10: In the center of each circle, spread an even layer of jam and mashed banana.
Step 11: Bring the edges of the dough up and lightly pinch them together around the fruit mixture.
Step 12: Bake the pastries for 25 to 30 minutes until golden brown.
Step 13: Let cool before serving.

**Nutrition Information**: (per serving)
Calories: 350, Total Fat: 17g, Saturated Fat: 10g, Trans Fat: 0g, Cholesterol: 50mg, Sodium: 220mg, Total Carbohydrates: 43g, Dietary Fiber: 2g, Sugars: 14g, Protein: 5g

## 84. Salted Caramel Chocolate Danish Pastries

Salted Caramel Chocolate Danish Pastries combine a creamy and salty caramel topping with a chocolate and pastry base for an indulgent and decadent treat.
Serving: 12 Danish pastries
Prep Time: 15 minutes
| Ready Time: 45 minutes

**Ingredients:**
- 3/4 cup vegan butter, divided
- 2 1/2 tablespoons all-purpose flour
- 2 tablespoons brown sugar
- Pinch of salt
- 1/2 teaspoon almond extract
- 2 packages puff pastry sheets, thawed
- 1/2 cup vegan semisweet chocolate chips

- 1/2 cup vegan salted caramel sauce

**Instructions:**
1. Preheat the oven to 375F.
2. In a small bowl, combine 1/4 cup vegan butter, flour, sugar, and salt until crumbly. Stir in almond extract until combined.
3. Unfold puff pastry sheets and lay them on a lightly floured surface. Spread the butter mixture on each pastry sheet. Sprinkle chocolate chips on one pastry sheet and salted caramel sauce over the other pastry sheet.
4. Top each pastry sheet with the other pastry sheet and press lightly so that the topping is distributed evenly. Cut into 12 equal pieces.
5. Place the pastries on an ungreased baking sheet and bake in preheated oven for 25-30 minutes, or until golden brown.
6. Remove from oven and brush the top of the pastries with remaining vegan butter.

**Nutrition Information:**
Calories: 250, Fat: 16g, Protein: 2g, Carbs: 29g, Fiber: 2g, Sugar: 13g, Sodium: 135mg

## 85. Creamy Custard Coconut Danish Pastries

Creamy Custard Coconut Danish Pastries are a delectable treat that can be enjoyed as an indulgent breakfast, special occasion dessert, or a tasty snack. Combining creamy custard, sweet coconut flakes, and light and fluffy pastries, this scrumptious treat is sure to satisfy even the most discerning palate.
Serving: 8-10 people
| Preparation Time: 1 hour
| Ready Time: 1 hour 15 minutes

**Ingredients:**
- 1 package puff pastry dough
- 4 large eggs
- 2 cups (400 ml) light cream
- 1/2 cup (100 g) sugar
- 1 teaspoon vanilla extract
- 2 tablespoons (25 g) cornstarch

- 2 cups (200 g) shredded coconut
- 2 tablespoons (30 g) butter
- 1 tablespoon (15 g) sugar

**Instructions:**
1. Preheat your oven to 350F (175°C). Line two baking sheets with parchment paper.
2. Unroll the puff pastry dough and cut it into 4-inch (10 cm) squares. Place the squares on the prepared baking sheets.
3. In a bowl, whisk together the eggs, cream, sugar, and vanilla extract until combined.
4. In a separate bowl, mix together the cornstarch and coconut flakes.
5. Divide the egg mixture and coconut mixture between the pastry squares, making sure to spread the mixture evenly.
6. Dot the pastries with the butter and sprinkle with the sugar.
7. Bake for 25-30 minutes until the pastries are golden brown.
8. Allow the pastries to cool before serving.

**Nutrition Information:**
Serving Size: 1 pastry
Calories: 250 kcal
Total Fat: 13 g
Saturated Fat: 5 g
Cholesterol: 76 mg
Sodium: 148 mg
Carbohydrate: 28 g
Fiber: 1 g
Sugar: 12 g
Protein: 7 g

## 86. Nutella-Raspberry Danish Pastries

The irresistible combination of nutella and raspberry melds together in this delicious and indulgent Nutella-Raspberry Danish Pastry.
Serving: 16 pastries
| Preparation Time: 30 minutes
| Ready Time: 1 hour 10 minutes

**Ingredients:**
- 1 17.3-ounce box of puff pastry sheets
- 1/2 cup of Nutella
- 16 raspberries, washed and dried
- 2 tablespoons of sugar
- 1 large egg, beaten

**Instructions:**
1. Preheat the oven to 375 degrees F.
2. Cut each pastry sheet into 4 separate squares.
3. Place 1-2 teaspoons of Nutella into the center of each square, top with a raspberry and sprinkle with sugar.
4. Fold all four sides of each square up, pinching the edges together to form a pocket.
5. Place pastries on a lightly greased or parchment paper-lined baking sheet, brush lightly with beaten egg.
6. Bake for 15-20 minutes or until pastries have puffed up and are lightly golden.
7. Serve warm and enjoy!

**Nutrition Information** (per pastry):
Calories: 127, Fat: 7.4 g, Sodium: 54 mg, Carbohydrates: 13.2 g, Protein: 1.7 g.

## 87. Caramel-Walnut Danish Pastries

This delectable Caramel-Walnut Danish Pastries recipe is perfect for indulging in a special breakfast treat or for an afternoon snack! The combination of rich caramel, crunchy walnuts and sweet, flaky pastry makes it a decadent treat.
Serving: Makes 12 danishes
| Preparation Time: 30 minutes
| Ready Time: 1 hour

**Ingredients:**
For the pastry
- 2 1/2 cups all-purpose flour
- 3 tablespoons sugar

- Pinch of salt
- 8 tablespoons cold cubed butter
- 1/2 cup cold water

For the filling
- 3/4 cup caramel sauce
- 1/2 cup chopped walnuts

**Instructions:**
1. Preheat oven to 375F (190°C).
2. In a large bowl, combine flour, sugar, and salt. Cut in the cold butter until the mixture resembles coarse crumbs. Stir in cold water until a dough forms.
3. Turn dough onto a lightly floured surface and roll out to a 14-inch square. Cut into 12 equal squares.
4. Place squares onto a baking sheet and spoon 1 tablespoon of caramel sauce and 1 tablespoon of walnuts onto each square.
5. Bring 2 opposite corners of the squares together to form a triangle and pinch together at the top.
6. Bake for 20 minutes or until golden brown.

**Nutrition Information:**
Calories: 157 kcal, Carbohydrates: 17 g, Protein: 3 g, Fat: 8 g, Saturated Fat: 4 g, Trans Fat: 0 g, Cholesterol: 15 mg, Sodium: 70 mg, Potassium: 34 mg, Fiber: 1 g, Sugar: 4 g, Vitamin A: 86 IU, Calcium: 15 mg, Iron: 1 mg

## 88. Apple Cider-Coconut Danish Pastries

A delicious combination of apple cider and coconut flavors, Apple Cider-Coconut Danish Pastries will make a delightful addition to any holiday meal. Enjoy a festive treat that you can make in no time.
Serving: 8-10
| Preparation Time: 15 minutes
| Ready Time: 45 minutes

**Ingredients:**
- 2 cups apples, peeled, cored, and diced small
- 1/2 cup brown sugar

- 1/2 cup chopped walnuts
- 1 cup apple cider
- 2 packages ready-made puff pastry dough, defrosted
- 1 cup dried coconut
- 2 tablespoons butter, melted
- Extra butter for brushing the pastries

**Instructions:**
1. Preheat oven to 375° Fahrenheit.
2. In a medium bowl, mix together apples, brown sugar, walnuts, and cider. Stir until ingredients are well combined.
3. Cut each puff pastry sheet into 4 small rectangles.
4. Place a spoonful of the apple mixture in the center of each pastry. Top with a sprinkle of coconut.
5. Fold top and bottom sides of pastry towards the center, and brush edges with melted butter.
6. Place danish pastries on a greased baking sheet and brush with extra melted butter.
7. Bake for 20-25 minutes, or until pastries are golden brown.

**Nutrition Information** (per serving):
Calories: 166, Fat: 8 g, Saturated Fat: 4 g, Sodium: 159 mg, Potassium: 79 mg, Carbohydrates: 20 g, Fiber: 1 g, Sugar: 8 g, Protein: 2 g

## 89. Honey-Lemon Danish Pastries

Enjoy a delicious and sweet treat with these Honey-Lemon Danish Pastries. Enjoy the goodness of honey, tang of lemon, and flaky pastry in every bite!
Serving: 8-10
| Preparation Time: 15 minutes
| Ready Time: 1 hour

**Ingredients:**
- 2/3 cup all-purpose flour
- 1/4 cup wheat flour
- 2 tablespoons white sugar
- 2 1/2 teaspoons active dry yeast

- 1/2 teaspoon salt
- 2 tablespoons butter, melted
- 2 tablespoons honey
- 2 tablespoons lemon juice
- 1 egg
- 1/4 cup powdered sugar
- 2 tablespoons honey

**Instructions:**
1. In a medium bowl, mix together the flours, sugar, yeast, and salt.
2. In a small bowl, mix together the melted butter, honey, and lemon juice.
3. Combine the wet ingredients with the dry ingredients and mix until a dough forms. Knead the dough for 3-5 minutes.
4. Place the dough in a greased bowl and cover with a damp cloth. Allow to rise in a warm place for 40 minutes.
5. Preheat the oven to 375F (190C).
6. Divide the dough into 8-10 pieces and roll each piece into a circle about 8 inches (20 cm) in diameter. Place the circles on an ungreased baking sheet.
7. Beat the egg and brush it over the top of each pastry.
8. Bake for 15-20 minutes or until golden brown.
9. Cool on a wire rack and dust with powdered sugar and honey.

**Nutrition Information:**
Total Fat: 4.2 g, Saturated Fat: 2.2 g, Trans Fat: 0.1 g, Cholesterol: 20.5 mg, Sodium: 150.4 mg, Total Carbohydrate: 46.6 g, Dietary Fiber: 2.0 g, Sugars: 19.2 g, Protein: 5.1 g

## 90. Mango-Coconut Danish Pastries

Mango-Coconut Danish Pastries are flaky, buttery pastries filled with sweet, tropical flavor. Layers of mango and coconut are wrapped in pastry dough for a delicious and unique breakfast treat. For a sweet start to the day, these pastry indulgences are sure to be a hit.
Serving: 8-10 pieces
| Preparation Time: 15 minutes
| Ready Time: 45 minutes

**Ingredients:**
- 1 1/2 cups all-purpose flour
- 1/4 cup granulated sugar
- 12 tablespoons unsalted butter, chilled and diced
- Pinch of salt
- 4-5 tablespoons ice cold water
- 2 cups diced fresh mango
- 1 cup shredded coconut

**Instructions:**
- Preheat oven to 375F.
- In a large bowl, combine flour, sugar, butter, and salt. Use a pastry cutter to cut the butter pieces into the flour until it resembles wet sand.
- Gradually add water to the mixture, stirring with a fork until it forms a soft dough.
- On a lightly floured surface, roll dough out into a large rectangle.
- Place diced mango and shredded coconut in a single layer on top of the dough.
- Roll the dough into a cylinder and cut into 8-10 sections.
- Place each section onto a parchment-lined baking sheet and brush with cold water.
- Bake for 35-45 minutes, or until pastry is golden-brown.
- Allow to cool before serving.

**Nutrition Information** (per serving):
- Calories: 280 kcal
- Fat: 11 g
- Carbohydrates: 39 g
- Protein: 3 g
- Sodium: 55 mg

## 91. Pecan-Cream Cheese Danish Pastries

Pecan-Cream Cheese Danish Pastries are a delightful pastry smothered in a rich cream cheese and pecan topping. They are easy to make and full of flavor!

Serving: 8-10 servings
| Preparation Time: 20 minutes
| Ready Time: 1 hour

**Ingredients:**
- 1 cup softened cream cheese
- 2 tablespoons of sugar
- 2 tablespoons of heavy cream
- 2/3 cup of chopped pecans
- 1 can (8-ounce) of refrigerated crescent roll
- 1/4 cup of melted butter

**Instructions:**
1. Preheat oven to 375F.
2. In a small bowl, beat cream cheese and sugar on medium until creamy. Add the heavy cream and beat until smooth. Stir in the chopped pecans.
3. Place the crescent roll dough in an ungreased 9-inch glass pie plate. Separate into the 8 triangles; press together at center to form a circle.
4. Spoon heaping tablespoonfuls of cream cheese mixture onto center of each dough triangle.
5. Brush dough triangle with melted butter.
6. Bring corners of dough up over filling and twist to close.
7. Bake 25-30 minutes or until golden brown.

**Nutrition Information:**
1 serving of Pecan-Cream Cheese Danish Pastries contains 341 calories, 21g fat, 25.9g carbohydrates, and 4.3g protein.

## 92. Jam-Filled Banana Danish Pastries

Jam-Filled Banana Danish Pastries are a delightful combination of light dough, sweet banana and gooey jams. These flaky pastries are sure to be a hit with the whole family.
Serving: Makes 12 danishes
| Preparation Time: 45 minutes
| Ready Time: 1 hour 15 minutes

**Ingredients:**

- 2 and 1/4 cups all-purpose flour
- 2 and 1/2 tablespoons active dry yeast
- 2 teaspoons granulated sugar
- 3/4 teaspoon salt
- 1/2 cup mashed banana (about 1 banana)
- 1/3 cup whole milk
- 1/3 cup butter, melted
- 1 egg
- 3/4 cup store-bought jam of choice
- 1 teaspoon butter
- 2 tablespoons confectioners' sugar

**Instructions:**
1. In a bowl, combine the flour, yeast, sugar, and salt.
2. In a separate bowl, combine the mashed banana, milk, melted butter, and egg.
3. Pour the wet ingredients into the dry ingredients, stirring until the dough is combined.
4. Turn the dough out onto a lightly floured surface and knead for 3-5 minutes.
5. Place the dough in a greased bowl and cover with a damp cloth. Let rise in a warm place for 45 minutes.
6. After rising, roll the dough out onto a lightly floured surface and cut 12 (3-inch) circles.
7. Place a tablespoon of jam in the middle of each circle and fold the sides up to form triangles.
8. Place the triangles onto a baking sheet lined with parchment paper and bake at 375F for 25-30 minutes, or until golden brown.
9. Remove the pastries from the oven and brush with melted butter.
10. Sprinkle with confectioners' sugar and serve.

**Nutrition Information:**
Serving size: 1 danish | Calories: 205 | Fat: 8g | Carbohydrates: 28g | Protein: 3.4g | Sugar: 12g | Sodium: 241mg

## 93. Caramel-Pecan Danish Pastries

Delicious, caramel-pecan Danish Pastries are the perfect way to start your day or as a bite-sized dessert. This recipe is sure to tantalize your taste buds with its mixture of sweet and salty flavors!
Serving: Makes 12 pastries
| Preparation Time: 30 minutes
| Ready Time: 2 hours

**Ingredients:**
1. 1 sheet of puff pastry
2. 1/2 cup of brown sugar
3. 1/2 cup of white sugar
4. 2 tablespoons of melted butter
5. 1 cup of chopped pecans
6. 1/2 teaspoon of salt

**Instructions:**
1. Preheat oven to 350 degrees F
2. Line a baking sheet with parchment paper and set aside
3. Cut the puff pastry sheet into 12 even squares and place on prepared baking sheet
4. In a small bowl, mix together sugars, melted butter, pecans and salt
5. Place a spoonful of the mixture onto each puff pastry square
6. Fold up two adjacent corners of the puff pastry to create a triangle, pressing firmly to seal around the edges
7. Place in preheated oven and bake for 15-20 minutes until golden brown
8. Allow to cool slightly before serving

**Nutrition Information** (per serving):
Calories: 204, Fat: 11.5g, Carbs: 23.5g, Protein: 2.6g

## 94. Vanilla-Ginger Danish Pastries

Vanilla-Ginger Danish Pastries are flaky, buttery pastries that are filled with a sweet vanilla and spicy ginger cream for a delicious combination.
Serving: 8 pastries
| Preparation Time: 10 minutes
| Ready Time: 30 minutes

**Ingredients:**
- 1 sheet of puff pastry, defrosted
- 1/4 cup (60g) mascarpone
- 3 tbsp (45ml) vanilla extract
- 4 tsp (30ml) ground ginger
- Powdered sugar, for dusting

**Instructions:**
1. Preheat oven to 375F (190°C).
2. Cut the pastry sheet into 8 equal rectangles, then transfer to a lined baking sheet.
3. In a small bowl, mix together the mascarpone, vanilla extract, and ground ginger, until creamy.
4. Spread the mascarpone mixture onto each pastry rectangle, then fold the edges of each pastry up over the filling and pinch closed.
5. Bake in preheated oven for 10-15 minutes, until golden brown.
6. Dust with powdered sugar and serve.

**Nutrition Information**: (Per Serving)
Calories: 160 kcal
Fat: 12 g
Carbohydrates: 9 g
Protein: 2.5 g
Sugars: 0.5 g

## 95. Orange-Cherry Danish Pastries

Enjoy a delightful sweet treat with this Orange-Cherry Danish Pastry recipe! This delectable pastry is dressed up with a sweet orange glaze, dried cherries, and a bit of almond extract to take it over the top.
Serving: 8
| Preparation Time: 20 minutes
| Ready Time: 30 minutes

**Ingredients:**
1. 1/2 cup unsalted butter, softened
2. 2 tablespoons granulated sugar

3. 2 teaspoons almond extract
4. 2 tablespoons orange juice
5. 1/2 cup dried cherries, chopped
6. 1/4 teaspoon salt
7. 1/4 teaspoon ground cinnamon
8. 1 sheet frozen puff pastry (1/2 of a 17.3-ounce package), thawed
9. 2 tablespoons apricot jam

**Instructions:**
1. Preheat the oven to 375F. Line a baking sheet with parchment paper.
2. In a medium bowl, cream together the butter and sugar until light and fluffy. Add the almond extract, orange juice, dried cherries, salt and cinnamon and mix until combined.
3. On a lightly floured surface, roll out the puff pastry into a 10x12-inch rectangle. Use a sharp knife or pizza cutter to cut the pastry into 4 rectangles, each about 10x3 inches in size.
4. Spread the butter mixture evenly over the pastry rectangles. Top each rectangle with a tablespoon of apricot jam.
5. Fold each rectangle in half and lightly crimp the edges to seal. Place on the prepared baking sheet and bake for 15 to 20 minutes, or until golden brown.
6. Cool for 5 minutes before serving warm.

**Nutrition Information:**
Calories: 283, Total Fat: 18 g, Saturated Fat: 8 g, Trans Fat: 0 g, Cholesterol: 19 mg, Sodium: 197 mg, Carbohydrates: 28 g, Fiber: 1 g, Sugar: 9 g, Protein: 2 g.

## 96. White Chocolate-Pecan Danish Pastries

White Chocolate-Pecan Danish Pastries provide a decadent combination of sweet and buttery pastry dough, gooey white chocolate pieces and crunchy, nutty pecans. They look impressive but require minimal effort to make.
Serving: Makes approximately 24 pastries
| Preparation Time: 20 minutes
| Ready Time: 1 hour

**Ingredients:**
1. 2 1/4 cups all-purpose flour
2. 1 1/4 teaspoons salt
3. 1 teaspoon granulated sugar
4. 2 sticks of salted butter, softened and cut into cubes
5. 1/2 cup very cold water
6. 1 cup white chocolate chips
7. 1 cup toasted pecans, finely chopped

**Instructions:**
1. In a medium bowl, whisk together the flour, salt and sugar. Using a pastry blender or two knives, cut the butter cubes into the flour mixture until the mixture is crumbly and there are no pieces of butter larger than a pea.
2. Add the cold water a couple of tablespoons at a time and mix together until the dough comes together. Knead a few times until the dough is smooth.
3. Wrap the dough tightly in plastic wrap and place in the refrigerator for a minimum of 30 minutes.
4. When you are ready to make the pastries, preheat the oven to 350F. Line a baking sheet with parchment paper.
5. On a lightly floured surface, roll out the dough to a 1/4-inch thickness. Using a round cookie cutter, cut out 24 circles from the dough.
6. Place the circles of dough onto the prepared baking sheet. Place 1 teaspoon of white chocolate chips and 1 teaspoon of chopped pecans into the center of each dough circle, taking care not to overfill the dough.
7. Fold the sides of the dough up and over the filling, pinching the corners together to form a shape resembling a Danish pastry.
8. Bake in the preheated oven for 15 minutes or until the pastries are golden brown.

**Nutrition Information:**
Serving size: 1 pastry / Calories: 157 / Fat: 9.5g / Saturated Fat: 5.2g / Cholesterol: 20.2mg / Sodium: 109mg / Carbohydrates: 15.7g / Dietary Fiber: 0.7g / Sugars: 5.6g / Protein: 2.1g

## 97. Pecan-Caramel Danish Pastries

This simple yet delicious pastry is sure to leave a lasting impression on any crowd! With a pecan-caramel filling and a golden pastry for the shell, these Pecan-Caramel Danish Pastries are a delightful treat for lovers of sweet desserts.

Serving: Makes 8 Danish pastries.
| Preparation Time: 25 minutes.
| Ready Time: 3 hours.

**Ingredients:**
- 2 sheets of store-bought Puff Pastry, thawed
- 1 1/2 cups of chopped Pecans
- 1 cup of light Brown Sugar
- 1/2 tsp of Vanilla Extract
- 2 tbsp of Butter, melted
- 2 Eggs
- 2 tbsp of All-purpose Flour
- 2 tbsp of Vegetable Oil

**Instructions:**
1. Preheat the oven to 375F (190°C).
2. In a medium bowl, mix together the pecans, brown sugar, vanilla, melted butter, eggs, and all-purpose flour until combined.
3. On a lightly floured surface, roll out one sheet of puff pastry. Cut out 8 (4-inch) circles and place them on a parchment paper-lined baking sheet.
4. Divide the pecan-caramel mixture onto the pastry circles.
5. Roll out the remaining sheet of pastry and cut out 8 (4-inch) circles. Place the pastry circles on top of the pastries with the pecan-caramel mixture. Using a fork, press around the edges to seal them.
6. Brush each pastry with vegetable oil and poke a few holes on top.
7. Bake for 18-20 minutes until golden brown.

**Nutrition Information:**
Per Serving: 203 calories; 9.5g fat; 23.8g carbohydrates; 4g protein.

# 98. Blueberry-Cream Cheese Danish Pastries

Mouthwatering and delicious, these Blueberry-Cream Cheese Danish Pastries are a beautiful breakfast treat or a savory-sweet snack. With an irresistible combination of cream cheese, blueberries, and a buttery pastry crust, you won't be able to resist these goodies.

Serving: 12 pastries
| Preparation Time: 25 minutes
| Ready Time: 35 minutes

**Ingredients:**
1. 1 package (8 ounces) cream cheese, softened
2. 2 tablespoons white sugar
3. 1 teaspoon pure vanilla extract
4. 1 package (15 ounces) prepared puff pastry, thawed
5. 1/4 cup almond paste
6. 1 teaspoon almond extract
7. 2/3 cup fresh blueberries
8. 1 beaten egg for glazing
9. 1/4 cup coarse sugar for finishing

**Instructions:**
1. Preheat oven to 350F. Grease a cookie sheet or line with parchment paper.
2. In a medium bowl, combine cream cheese, sugar, and vanilla extract; mix until creamy. Set aside.
3. On a lightly floured surface, roll out puff pastry into an approximate 10-inch square. Cut into 12 equal triangles.
4. Spread cream cheese mixture onto each triangle. Roll up lightly, starting at the wide end and ending at the tip.
5. Place dough on greased cookie sheet.
6. In a small bowl, mix almond paste and almond extract together. Cut into small pieces and sprinkle over each pastry.
7. Top with blueberries, then lightly brush with beaten egg.
8. Sprinkle with coarse sugar.
9. Bake for 25 minutes or until golden brown.

**Nutrition Information:**
Calories: 316; Total Fat: 19.4g; Cholesterol: 42mg; Sodium: 172mg; Total Carbohydrates: 28.2g; Protein: 5.3g.

## 99. Maple-Bacon Danish Pastries

This decadent pastry combines the salty and sweet flavors of bacon and maple for an irresistible combination. Enjoy a slice of the heavenly Maple-Bacon Danish Pastries for a delightful breakfast or brunch.
Serving: 8-10
| Preparation Time: 30 minutes
| Ready Time: 1 hour

### Ingredients:
1. 1package (3 ounces) cream cheese, softened
2. 3 tablespoons maple-flavored syrup
3. 3 tablespoons finely chopped cooked bacon
4. 1 package refrigerated reduced fat crescent dinner rolls
5. 2 tablespoons cornflake crumbs

### Instructions:
1. Preheat oven to 375 degrees F.
2. In a small bowl, beat cream cheese, syrup, and bacon until blended.
3. Unroll crescent dough; separate into 8 triangles.
4. Spread 1 tablespoon cream cheese mixture over each triangle.
5. Roll up each triangle, beginning at short end; place on a ungreased baking sheet.
6. Sprinkle with cornflake crumbs.
7. Bake for 13-17 minutes or until golden brown.

### Nutrition Information:
per serving (1 pastry): 120 calories, 5g total fat, 2.5g saturated fat, 160mg sodium, 17g carbohydrates, 0g dietary fiber, 4g protein.

# CONCLUSION

The success of the Cookbook 99 Delicious Danish Pastry Recipes: A Sweet Taste of Denmark is evident in providing a collection of scrumptious recipes for all to enjoy. The Danish pastry style is unique and is sure to add a unique touch to any baking enthusiast's repertoire. From basic techniques for preparing buttery dough, to assembling rich and fluffy treats, this cookbook demystifies the process of creating delectable Danish pastries. By showcasing recipes from all over the world, the book highlights the best in this particular genre of pastry dishes.

Danish pastries may look intimidating to some, but with the help of this book, even the novice baker will find themselves confidently whipping up all sorts of mouthwatering Danish creations. Intertwined with the recipes, are snippets of the history and culture of Denmark and the unique techniques that make this particular pastry special.

Whether you're looking for delicate, flaky, layered pastries, or chewy, soft, bready treats, the Cookbook 99 Delicious Danish Pastry Recipes provides it all. The varied selection of ingredients and techniques makes it easy to bring Danish pastries to any table. With this book, you now have a sweet taste of Denmark right in your home. Give it a try and you will not be disappointed.

Printed in Great Britain
by Amazon